FRENCH LEGISLATORS, 1800-1834

FRENCH LEGISLATORS, 1800-1834

A Study in Quantitative History

Thomas D. Beck

UNIVERSITY OF CALIFORNIA PRESS
Berkeley • Los Angeles • London
1974

University of California Press
Berkeley and Los Angeles, California
University of California Press, Ltd.
London, England

Copyright © 1974 by The Regents of the University of California

ISBN: 0–520–02535–0
Library of Congress Catalog Card Number: 73–83059
Printed in the United States of America

For Martha

CONTENTS

PREFACE

Since this is quantitative history, my first thank you should be to the machines that made this study possible—but this is as unnecessary as thanking one's notefile or typewriter. I have written a quantitative history and hopefully the numbers are accurate, since everything flows from this basic premise. Like most historians, however, I have had to ask the questions and order the information so that it made sense. Often more questions are raised than answers are provided; I believe this is one of the chief values of quantitative studies. The answers that have been provided deal with limited questions, and even though I draw some general conclusions from the total study I do not believe that I have found *the* answer to the history of this period. Much more study must support my findings, but I do present my results with the belief that others will find supportive evidence.

I am indebted to many people for their help in this undertaking. It began as a seminar paper for Richard Herr in Winter/Spring 1968 when it included only the elections of 1827 to 1834. Reaching its present dimensions as my dissertation, again under the most intelligent guidance of Richard Herr, it was finally refined during the leisure provided by the current employment situation. I want to thank the Institute of International Studies for the money that enabled me to be in France in 1969–1970, Margaret Baker at the Survey Research Center and Michael Tiktinsky of the Psychology Department for help with the computer programming, and Gerald Cavanaugh and Ernst Haas for helpful suggestions—all of these from the University of California, Berkeley. My greatest thanks go to my wife for suggesting the use of factor analysis and for bringing clarity out of my often confused syntax.

The errors are my own. For those who want to draw their own conclusions, I have provided as much data as possible in the appendixes, and by writing to me the raw data on the deputies can be called forth from the computer.

I

INTRODUCTION

Except for the reign of Napoleon, the first third of the nineteenth century is probably one of the least studied periods of French history. The Revolution of 1789 and the decade following have been minutely analyzed, but the period after 1815 has often been viewed as unexciting and unworthy of attention. Fortunately this view is changing, since today historians can see that the Revolution may have destroyed the Old Regime, but it did not reconstitute society. Although Alfred Cobban contends that no reconstitution was necessary,[1] most historians would disagree. Emmanuel Beau de Loménie, speaking from the despair of Vichy, looked back to the Eighteenth of Brumaire to explain the Fall of France. To Beau de Loménie the bourgeoisie[2] had consolidated their position at this time with their sponsorship of Napoleon Bonaparte, and they were not to relinquish this position throughout the century.[3] Georges Lefebvre saw the Eighteenth of Brumaire in the same manner, for in his interpretation the Revolution had destroyed the nobility and placed the bourgeoisie at the top of society.[4]

Other historians do not agree as to which social groups dominated the early years of the nineteenth century. Since Napoleon

[1] Alfred Cobban, *The Social Interpretation of the French Revolution* (Cambridge, 1965).

[2] See chap. 2 on methodology for my definition of *bourgeoisie*. Here I am using the term as it is employed by Beau de Loménie in the work cited in note 3.

[3] Emmanuel Beau de Loménie, *Les résponsabilités des dynasties bourgeoises* (Paris, 1943).

[4] Georges Lefebvre, *Napoléon* (Paris, 1965), pp. 64–65.

was unable to maintain himself in power, France experienced
the restoration of the Bourbons. To some this equaled the return
of the Old Regime; such an occurrence caused historians such as
Jean Lhomme and Felix Ponteil to believe the emergence of the
bourgeoisie occurred only after 1830.[5] André Tudesq also believes that a new group began to dominate society during the
July Monarchy, but to him this new group was broader than
just the bourgeoisie.[6] Tudesq's view is therefore closer to the
opinion of Sherman Kent, which is that the large landowners
continued in control.[7] These contradictory opinions present at
least three problems: what was the meaning of the return of the
Bourbons, what were the consequences of the Revolution of
1830, and, if it is possible to deduce social class dominance from
political history, then what was the true social reality of the
period? By studying a particular group in this society I hope to
contribute to the solutions of these problems.

In selecting an institution whose membership could be analyzed it was necessary to find one that was important and also
one that represented the society in some manner. Although the
elected legislators were chosen by a limited suffrage, a prima
facie case for them is obvious—they were the national legislature
and they were the representatives of the nation. The matter of
their importance is more open to question. Doubtless, the legislature under Napoleon, the Corps Législatif, was not an influential body.[8] However, its small amount of political power does
not negate the fact that its members were chosen to represent an
economically and socially important section of society, and these
men did derive a certain amount of status from their positions.
As for the legislatures of the Restoration and the July Monarchy,
their importance is well established.[9] They became the main

[5] Jean Lhomme, *La grande bourgeoisie au pouvoir, 1830–1880*; (Paris,
1960); Felix Ponteil, *Les institutions de la France de 1814 à 1870* (Paris,
1966).

[6] André-Jean Tudesq, *Les grands notables en France, 1840–1848* (Paris,
1964).

[7] Sherman Kent, *Electoral Procedures under Louis-Philippe* (New Haven,
1937).

[8] Jacques Godechot, *Les institutions de la France sous la Révolution et
l'Empire* (Paris, 1968), p. 583.

[9] Paul Bastid, *Les institutions politiques de la monarchie parlementaire
française, 1814–1848* (Paris, 1954).

forum for political debate and, although policy was decided by
the King and his ministers, the Chamber of Deputies had considerable power—as for example when the chamber's intransi-
gence in the face of Charles X led to the Revolution of 1830.
Finally, there is sufficient documentation on the legislators to
allow them to be studied.[10]

An investigation of the legislators also allows me to examine
certain other questions: the effects of the various electoral laws
as well as the consequences of the changes that were made in
them during the period. The basic franchise system was a limited one, but there were important modifications in 1820 and
1830. The effects of these changes have often been assumed from
the evidence of just one election. I cover the entire period and
evaluate the results of the changed laws in comparison to other
changes that took place at the same time.

I also explore the question of regionalism in France by studying various aspects of the regions which the different types of
legislators represented. I have characterized the departments of
France for their social, economic, and demographic aspects, so
I can compare the type of department and the type of legislator
in a statistical manner. This correlation analysis permits more
than a purely political evaluation of regionalism and also offers
some new insights into the Restoration and the causes of the
Revolution of 1830.

Although it comes toward the end of the period I am studying, the Revolution of 1830 is the focal center of my work. The
entire project was conceived in an attempt to analyze the consequences of that revolution. I cast my study back in time in order
to achieve a perspective that would allow for the recognition
and assessment of social change. The Napoleonic period provides a convenient introduction to the period of constitutional
monarchy and is an important period in its own right, and the
Restoration itself was the breeding ground for the Revolution
of 1830. I conclude my study after the election of 1834, because
the new regime was firmly established by that time.[11]

In describing the changes that took place from 1800 to 1834

[10] *Archives nationales*, Séries C1164–C1323, CC28–CC49, FicII, and FicIII.
Also see Bibliography: *Dictionaries*.

[11] Jean Vidalenc, *Le département de l'Eure sous la monarchie constitutionnelle, 1814–1848* (Paris, 1952), p. 330.

the concept of the New France holds a prominent place. The New France is the France that emerges from the Revolution. We know that the post-Revolutionary France was not a dynamic capitalist society like the one developing in England, but neither was it the Old France of the *ancien régime*. The Revolution destroyed the old legal classes, the remnants of the artisan guilds, and the special privileges of the Church, and it established civil rights and constitutionalism. Heredity and traditions were reduced and wealth and current position were raised as factors for determining social status. These social changes particularly affected the upper classes and the lack of effect on the peasant class did not alter the consequences for the upper classes. The Revolution was the great experiment, and it was the outcome of that experiment which concerned the men of the early nineteenth century: the New France is the beneficiary of the destruction of the old traditions. In the most general terms, the New France is the France where there is legal equality, freedom, and a constitution, where careers are open to talent, and where wealth and not just birth counts. The Napoleonic period was the first time the New France consolidated its hold after the experiment, and it is under the July Monarchy that the New France wins completely. Then the debate in politics shifts from whether the experiment should succeed to how far should the experiment be carried.

The Revolution of 1830 thus draws together many of the crucial questions in which I am interested: how "bourgeois" was the July Monarchy, what was the effect of the changes in the electoral laws, how important was regionalism, and just what type of men were elected? With these questions in front of me, I undertook the study of all of the legislators elected from the Eighteenth of Brumaire until the end of 1834.

Two thousand eight hundred sixty-two individuals held office in this period, and I preferred to use quantitative methods in order to handle the data. I chose to use this methodology, which often loses sight of the individual, because I feel that the rule of completeness is a more satisfying method of describing an institution than the "typical case" approach so often employed by historians. By including all of those elected over a considerable period of time, I could go beyond the use of either a few prominent men or a single election to characterize a period. Also I was able to achieve a perspective from which to view the less critical elections and therefore to ascertain if they were really as unimportant as previously thought.

Both quantitative and social history are particularly dependent on the definition of terms; without some agreement on my definitions and methodology little of what I discover will carry any significance. Thus my first task is to explain my methodology.

II

METHODOLOGY

In undertaking a quantitative history, the methods of handling the data often predetermine the results. My aim in defining terms and quantifying information is to develop the categories most useful to elucidating the society and politics of the first third of the nineteenth century in France. The five areas in which methodology is critical to this analysis are the social class, the occupation, the experience, and the party affiliation of the deputies, and the social-economic-demographic characterizations of the departments.

A great deal of controversy exists on methods of defining social groups.[1] Although the categorizing of persons is somewhat arbitrary and is done by and for the benefit of the historian, I cannot agree with the philosophy of men like Richard Cobb who say that all categorizing is artificial.[2] By grouping people the historian is only doing what all societies have done in trying to explain their behavior. The crucial requirement is that the categories make sense to the participants in the events being analyzed and are helpful to the historian in understanding the situation.

Because most of the deputies were men of substantial wealth and, therefore, in the upper strata of society, the definitions of

---

[1] For example see Lenore O'Boyle, "The Middle Class in Western Europe, 1815–1848," *American Historical Review* 71 (April 1966), and Alfred Cobban, "The 'Middle Class' in France, 1815–1848," *French Historical Studies* 5 (Spring 1967).

[2] Richard Cobb, *The Police and The People: French Popular Protest, 1789–1820* (Oxford, 1970).

my social groups are much easier than if the entire spectrum of society had to be classified. Nevertheless, the problem is still a difficult one, but it can be greatly simplified by not trying to arrive at one label for each individual, since the deputies need to be evaluated on both a basis for the Old Regime and a basis for the New France. "Social class," therefore, denotes the grouping for the Old Regime and "Occupation" denotes the grouping for the New France.

The categories of Social class are based on the legal definition of orders during the Old Regime. This immediately yields two groups, the nobility and the roturiers, but certain modifications are necessary. One type of man, the "Imperial noble," which includes all men ennobled by Napoleon—even including men of the nobility of the Old Regime—must be separated from both groups and given its own category of Social class. The remaining nobility and roturiers are each divided into two groups, the nobility into "Titled" and "Nontitled," the roturiers into "Near nobles" and "Bourgeois."

A further problem arises among the nobility in trying to distinguish between the bonafide nontitled noble and the man who has assumed his noble status on his own initiative by using the particle "de" in his name. From the birth certificate of the legislator it is possible to see if the father had used the particle "de," and if he had, it is an indication of Nontitled noble status. If this source is inconclusive, the legitimacy of the assumption of noble status can often be found in biographical material. Without either source to expose the false noble, men with the particle "de" are assumed to be Nontitled nobility.

The division of the roturiers into the two categories Near noble and Bourgeois reflects the difference between those who had noble pretensions and the bulk of the Third Estate. The Near noble includes both the deputies whose use of the particle "de" was illegitimate and the deputies who were likely to have achieved noble status if the Revolution had not intervened. The occupations of *avocat au parlement, conseiller du roi,* or *trésorier de France,* or a father listed on the birth certificate as a *seigneur, ecuyer,* or *rentier,* distinguishes the deputy who was close to noble status, and this deputy is thus included in the Near noble category. The Bourgeois category encompasses all the remaining roturiers. The term bourgeois was chosen because it correctly reflects what these men were or would have been under the Old Regime—wealthy, honored, urban notables.[3] The Marxian definition in particular or any other post-Revolution definition of bourgeois should not be substituted if one wants to correctly understand this analysis. The fact that the term bourgeois changes its meaning is part of the story of this period.[4]

The Social class category measures a man's place in the Old France as based on a legal definition of the Estates. A separate classification, Occupation, measures a man's place in the New France. Because of the large number of men in the study and the ensuing difficulty of determining and quantifying each man's lifestyle or class consciousness, the use of a sophisticated classification is not possible. A man's occupation, which avoids these problems, therefore reflects a deputy's position in early nineteenth-century French society.

The Occupation category measures both how a man earned his income and how he spent his nonleisure time. Income is not the only criterion, because a man's attitude toward politics is not determined solely by where his money came from; how a man spent his day is also important in determining what his political outlook would be. This is especially true in a period where many of the men in the upper classes call themselves *propriétaires*, a label often used as a status symbol as well as an accurate description of one's source of income. The use of the term *propriétaire* as a status symbol can be overcome by using the receipts of the deputy's tax payments to establish his source of income and by investigating his earlier career to see if it identified him as having been engaged in an active occupation.

Even when the source of income and how a man spent his time coincided, there can still be a problem in placing a man in an occupation category. For instance, if a man had more than

[3] Maurice Agulhon, *La vie sociale en Provence intérieure au lendemain de la Révolution* (Paris, 1970), pp. 103–108, 481–484; Régine Robin, *La société française en 1789: Semur-en-Auxois* (Paris, 1970), pp. 15–58; D. Roche and M. Vovelle, "Bourgeois, Rentiers, and Property Owners: Elements for Defining a Social Category at the End of the Eighteenth Century," in *New Perspectives on the French Revolution* (New York, 1965).

[4] Shirley Gruner, "The Revolution of July 1830 and the Expression 'Bourgeoisie,' " *The Historical Journal* 11 (1968).

one occupation, in which category should he be placed? The solution is to place him in the occupation in which he spent the greater part of his life. The final decision, however, is subjective, since the ultimate criterion is which occupation best represents the man when he was a deputy, and therefore a strict mathematical equation is not used to place the deputy in a category.

There are six general categories for Occupation:[5] (1) "Military," which includes all active military personnel as well as retired personnel who spent a significant part of their lives in the military; (2) "Law," which includes the legal professions, with *avocats* composing the great majority of this group; (3) "Professions," which includes all men outside the legal field who made their living from a mental skill acquired through advanced formal training; (4) "Business," which includes commerce, manufacturing, industry, and banking; (5) "Government," which includes the holders of a paid government post, with slightly over half of these in the magistrature (if a man held a government post only briefly and his usual occupation is known, he is not included in this group); and (6) "Proprietors," which includes all those identified as such, farmers (of which there were few), and all other men without an identifiable active occupation to fill their time.

The definition of occupation serves to measure both economic and personal interests, but since all of the men studied are wealthy, the level of income is not a criterion for the Occupation category. A separate category records the wealth of the deputies, and wealth is measured by the direct taxes they paid.[6]

The third area where methodology is critical is the quantification of the experience of the legislators. I define "Experience" as the holding of a government post. My particular method of quantification is to classify the type of public offices held by the

[5] See Appendix A for the complete list of occupations for each category.

[6] I have not tried to estimate a specific level of wealth from a deputy's taxes, since this is difficult if not impossible, but I employ the raw taxes paid as an estimate of wealth. Others have estimated taxes at approximately one-seventh of a man's income. See Nicolas Richardson, *The French Prefectoral Corps, 1814–1830* (Cambridge, 1966), pp. 158–160, and P. Bouyaux, "Les 'six cents plus imposés' du département de la Haute-Garonne en l'An X," *Annales du Midi* 70 (July 1958): 320.

deputies into separate categories and to divide time into various periods. The government posts are easy to divide into types. There is "Military," which includes both the navy and the army. All of the experience of the legislators was as officers, except a few who began in the ranks but quickly won a commission. The next type is "Magistrature," which includes all judicial posts except the local Justice of the Peace, whose duties made him more a member of the local administration than of the judiciary. "Administration," the third type of experience, is divided into three levels: "National," "Intermediate," and "Local." The time classification follows the traditional one of Old Regime, Revolution, Napoleonic, One Hundred Days, Restoration, and July Monarchy. Further subdivision proved fruitful only during the Restoration, where 1815, 1816–1819, and 1820–1830 are given separate periods to coincide with the politics of the government.

The result, then, is five different categories for eight different time periods. Not all of the data fit within this framework, however.[7] Unfortunately for historians who use quantification, man does not live in such simple categories and periods. A discussion of the sources of the data demonstrates how the final schema for Experience was constructed.

The basic source of information on the legislators is their electoral result forms, which are on deposit in the *Archives nationales*.[8] These forms give the winner of the election, his birth certificate, and the receipts of his tax payments, and they list his qualifications and the vote totals. This source is nearly 100 percent complete for the Restoration and the July Monarchy, but it is only about 60 percent complete prior to the Restoration. Supplementing this information are contemporary bio-dictionaries of the individual assemblies, of which there are at least two for each assembly beginning in 1815.[9] Beyond these there are the general bio-dictionaries and for the better-known deputies there are biographies, memoirs, and autobiographies— but these were not employed because for all the socioeconomic categories my information was complete for the well-known legislators, and therefore further investigation was redundant,

[7] See Appendix A for complete schema on Government Experience.
[8] *Archives nationales*, C1164–C1323 for May 1815 forward, and CC28–CC49 for information on candidates to the Corps Législatif.
[9] See Bibliography: *Dictionaries*.

and using noncomparable sources would have overweighted the better-known men.

These sources helped to dictate my time classification, since the bio-dictionaries follow the practice of reviewing a man's career by the traditional periods of history. Also this division of time often reflected what happened in practice; men gained and lost positions with the change in regimes. Dividing the Napoleonic period in half and also having a separate period for the First Restoration proved unsuccessful, because neither provided any additional information.

The categories of positions held by the deputies created the first serious roadblock in my quantification schema. How can a man who held posts in two categories in the same time period be classified? This problem does not arise with enough frequency to require any additional categories. For those cases that do occur, the deputies are categorized by a flexible standard based upon the importance of the position and the length of time each post was held. The object is always to try to best represent the experience of the legislator in terms of its probable effect on his future conduct. For example, if a man was a mayor of his home city and then received a prefecture, he is classified as a prefect since his experience as a prefect would probably be more influential on his behavior both as a candidate and as a member of the legislature. The most frequent overlap in positions held is between Local Administration, which is the least important type of position, and the other four, and in this case both positions are not reflected. The man is categorized in only the more important position. The Local Administration category, therefore, does not represent the extent of local officials who were deputies; it represents the number of legislators who were only local officials. In the other categories there is very little switching between categories even in different time periods. In other words, if a man began a career in the magistrature, he tended to remain there.

The eight time periods are adequate for the holding of government posts, but they are inadequate with respect to two important experiences of these years: emigration during the Revolution and opposition to the return of Napoleon. Therefore these two experiences are given special categories. Emigration is classified according to length and according to whether a man had fought against France. Opposition to the return of Napoleon in 1815 is defined as having emigrated during that time, as having resigned one's post by refusing to swear to the *Acte additionale*, or as having opposed his return publicly.[10]

The last area of definitions concerning the characteristics of the deputies is their party affiliation. In the Napoleonic period including the One Hundred Days the legislature had no power and therefore no parties existed, but during the Restoration and the July Monarchy this was no longer true. I use the term party to describe the political groupings of the deputies, but there were no cohesive or organized groups of deputies or voters. What organization there was usually formed around individuals. Nevertheless, because the Chambers of the Restoration and the July Monarchy held a considerable amount of political power, the attitude of the deputies was important, and thus it is possible to arrange the deputies into progovernment and antigovernment groupings. It is these groupings I call parties.

In trying to determine the party in which a man should be placed, it is not possible to investigate his votes on various issues since these votes were secret. Also, electioneering was considered inappropriate behavior, at least until the end of the Restoration, so no campaign literature is available. This lack of knowledge, however, is overcome by the use of the bio-dictionaries whose primary function had been to identify the political position of the deputies. The groupings I originally used followed a variety of patterns for the various legislatures. For instance, in 1815 there were the Ministerial Minority and the Majority, and in 1827 there were seven groupings based upon Left-Right labels and whether one voted among the 221 who rejected the king's address of March 1830. These designations were pooled into government and antigovernment parties. There was always one government party, the Left in 1815, the Center in 1816–1819, and the Right in 1820–1834, and usually two antigovernment parties, the Right in 1815–1819, the Left in 1816–1834, and the Extreme Right in 1824–1834. Doubtless the progovernment and antigovernment labels do some violence to those who were truly independent, but it was this difference that was critical in the politics of the time and I feel it reflects the realities of the situation more accurately than an attempt to

[10] See Appendix A for full details.

place the deputies in the smaller groupings where the fine differences would lead to a much greater probability of error.[11]

The important parties are the Left and the Right and each has a separate philosophy for the Restoration and the July Monarchy. The same labels are used because their basic attitude toward the government and toward each other was maintained and these were the designations of the contemporaries. The Left and the Right of the Restoration were divided by their views of the Revolution; the Left and the Right of the July Monarchy were divided by their views of the settlement of 1830. The Restoration Left favored the basic achievements of the Revolution of civil rights, representative government, and freedom— the attributes of the New France; the Right opposed the Revolutionary settlement. When the Right did favor representative government it was only a device to maintain the old elites in power. The key issues of the Restoration were all political in nature; the press laws and the electoral laws were the most divisive between the two groups, with the concern for the settlement of the national lands not far behind. These issues represented the shift in power from the Second to the Third Estate, and thus many social issues were translated into political ones. Economic issues, however, were not important in dividing the deputies.

After the Revolution of 1830 the Revolution was no longer the dividing line, since it was finally accepted by the vast majority of the population. The Right of the July Monarchy favored the limited results of the July revolution and the Left advocated a continuation of the revolution. Also, at this time the Left seemed to favor a more energetic policy, if in words only, as in its desire for a more forceful foreign policy than the government was pursuing. The divisive issues continued to be political, with press laws and restrictions on freedom very prominent; economic issues had more visibility than during the Restoration, but they still were not a basic factor in determining

[11] In his current work on the election of 1827 Sherman Kent has used labels similar to mine, and in my review of his work I found only 8 cases out of 430 where we had a significant difference. For complete details on the party groupings see Appendix A. I want to thank him for making his manuscript, which is soon to be published by Harvard University Press under the title *The Election of 1827 in France*, available to me.

the progovernment and antigovernment parties. The Right, therefore, was the conservative party, the Left the progressive party. At times these philosophies became reactionary or revolutionary, but such distinctions were likely to be a matter of opinion.

The fifth area where methodology is important involves the departments of France and is handled in the next chapter; this chapter deals only with the methodological problems of the legislators. For the readers who want more details, the entire coding system can be found in Appendix A.

III

MODERNIZATION AND POLITICAL OPINION

The object of characterizing the deputies is to determine if this process can teach us something about the first third of the nineteenth century. The deputies, however, are not the only aspect of the political system which can be profiled. The districts that elected the deputies also are capable of being characterized.

France has long been viewed as having two halves: the dynamic North and the static South with the dividing line running from Saint Malo to Geneva.[1] If the factors that made an area dynamic or static can be measured, then it can be determined if there is a correlation between these characteristics and the political opinion of the deputies who were elected from the same areas. This effort creates a methodological problem and it involves the utilization of a more complex statistical analysis than is undertaken in analyzing the characteristics of the deputies.

First the various areas of France have to be characterized. Even though it would have been better to use the individual electoral districts when these were employed,[2] since many departments had wide variations in their types of areas, I chose the department as the unit of analysis because it is only at this

[1] Le Baron Charles Dupin, *Forces productives et commerciales de la France* (Bruxelles, 1828).

[2] Individual districts were used for electing 258 of 430 deputies from 1820 to 1830 and for all of the deputies in 1831 and 1834.

level that the necessary information is available. An index of
factors which could distinguish those departments that were
modernizing from the more static ones was the ideal I sought,
but this ideal was beyond the data. Instead, 16 variables on the
social, economic, and demographic aspects of each department
were chosen to provide a profile of the type of area each department represented.[3]

The two social variables measured are the number of students
in secondary schools per 10,000 inhabitants in 1832[4] and the
percent of army recruits who could read in 1827–1829.[5] The six
economic variables are the number of *patentes*, a license to en-
gage in commercial activity, in 1838,[6] the number of industrial
workers in establishments with over 10 employees in 1847,[7]
the amount of industrial production in 1850,[8] the total agricultural revenue in 1812,[9] the agricultural yield per hectare in
1812,[10] and a composite of meat, wine, wool, and grain production in 1812.[11] The six demographic variables are the absolute
population size in 1821,[12] the percent of the change in the population between 1821 and 1836,[13] the population density in 1821,[14]

[3] I arrived at these variables through a general appreciation of mod-
ernization and a search of the available data. The inclusion of data from
outside the period is not by choice, but of necessity. The use of data on
1838 for *patentes* is not a problem if one considers the slight economic
changes in this period. The data on industry is a problem; see later in this
chapter for a discussion of it. The idea for the addition of the education
variables came from a colloquium given by Emmanuel Le Roy Ladurie at
Berkeley in 1967.

[4] *Statistique de l'enseignement primaire* (Paris, 1880), pp. 76–78.

[5] Ibid., pp. 340–343.

[6] *Statistique de la France: Industrie* (Paris, 1852), 1:268, 2:208, 3:240,
4:200.

[7] Ibid., 4:361–366.

[8] Ibid. The "total" figures were used.

[9] Le Comte Chaptal, *De l'industrie française* (Paris, 1819).

[10] Ibid.

[11] In order to balance the acreage needed to produce an equal value
of produce, which would measure the importance of agriculture to the department, I took grain acreage at full value, multiplied wine acreage by five
since it had a much greater yield per acre, multiplied meat acreage by two,
and divided wool acreage by three; then I added them together to produce
a total for my factor of agricultural production, which is a measure of
acreage devoted to agriculture.

[12] *Statistique de l'enseignement*, pp. 2–5.

[13] Ibid.   [14] Ibid., p xxxiv.

population over 10,000 in communes of 10,000 or more people in 1821, the percent of the change in the population over 10,000 in communes of 10,000 or more between 1821 and 1836, and the percent urban, which is defined as the population living in towns of more than 2,000 persons, in 1831.[15] Two final variables measure the wealth of the departments as judged by the number of registered voters in 1817 and again in 1831.[16]

The data on the economic factors needs to be interpreted in two ways: as a measure of current economic activity and as a measure of the changes that were occurring or were about to occur. The *Patente* is a measure of commercial activity during the period 1815–1834 even though the data is from 1838, since the changes in the distribution of commercial activity are not very great in this period. The agricultural factors are the most open to suspicion. The *Agricultural production* variable is only a rough estimate of the importance of agriculture to a department in 1812. *Agricultural revenue* and *Agricultural yield,* on the other hand, measure wealth rather than a type of economic activity. The data on the *Industrial workers* and *Industrial production* come from well beyond the period when the deputies were elected, and thus these data should be interpreted as indicating those areas that were or were soon to be modernizing. They should not be read as indicating any working class influence on the voters.

In order to analyze these data on the departments it is necessary to have a variable to test them against. The political opinion of the deputies provides the most useful variable and this means that the analysis can occur only for the elections from August 1815 to 1834, because there were no party groupings under Napoleon. The political opinion of each department is obtained for each election by determining what percentage of the departmental delegation is in each party. Each election needs just one measure of the results unless there are more than two parties for that election; when there are only two parties, then the percent of one party can be determined from the other. This occurred in 1815, 1820, 1821–1822, and 1824. There is an Extreme Right party in 1824, but because it was created after the election it is

[15] The figures for these last three variables were kindly supplied by Professor Charles Tilly.

[16] Paul Meuriot, *La population et les lois électorales en France de 1789 à nos jours* (Nancy, 1916), pp. 34–40.

included in the Right in measuring the election result itself. In 1816 and 1817–1819 there are three parties and thus each has to have a separate measure, and in 1827, 1830, 1831, and 1834 when the Extreme Right is too small to make having its own measure feasible, the Right and the Left also each have their own measure.

Once the data on the departments were collected[17] two types of statistical analyses were performed. First, Pearson correlation coefficients were computed on the 16 social-economic-demographic (hereafter SED) variables and the 22 measures for the political opinion variable.[18] These coefficients determine if there is any relationship between the variables, but they say nothing about cause and effect. In correlation analysis each pair of variables is compared along their entire length to see if there is a relationship between them. A measure of the relationship is given in terms of a number that ranges from 1.00 to –1.00. A figure of 1.00 means that an increase in one variable is always accompanied by a proportional increase in the other, and a figure of –1.00 means that an increase in one is accompanied by a proportional decrease in the other. A figure of 0.00 means that there is no relationship between the two variables being tested. Since these simple results are seldom obtained, it is up to the researcher to interpret the significance of the results.[19]

There are mathematical guides to interpretation which are utilized to discover the role that chance may have played in the results. I decided to use the 5-percent significance level, which means that the results would occur by chance less than 5 percent of the time—so given the sample size of 86 departments, and a coefficient whose lower confidence boundary was greater than 0.005,[20] a correlation of greater than 0.225 is considered to be significant.[21]

The second method of analysis performed was cluster analysis.

[17] See Appendix B, table 1, for the complete set of data.

[18] See Appendix B, table 4, for the complete correlation matrix.

[19] Edwin E. Ghiselli, *The Theory of Psychological Measurement*, (New York, 1964), pp. 101–118.

[20] I chose this figure to make certain that the significant figures would always be positive; despite its very low level, I feel it has meaning in this type of study.

[21] Helen M. Walker and Joseph Lev, *Elementary Statistical Methods* (New York, 1958), p. 261. At the 2 percent level the significant figure would be greater than 0.255 and for 1 percent it would be greater than 0.280.

This is an attempt to see if the variables will group together in clusters so that fewer variables will explain all of the relationships between the variables, that is, explain the entire correlation matrix.[22] This is done by recognizing that the variables have certain properties in common. This communality can be measured and through various statistical methods those variables whose correlations are most collinear with each other can be grouped into clusters. A cluster, then, is formed with certain limiting criteria by those variables that have high similarities within the group and high differences outside the group. Since the clusters can themselves be correlated with each variable independently, clustering proves to be a valuable method of summarizing the results of the statistical analyses.

The results of the correlation analysis made it possible to refine the original 16 SED variables. When two variables have high (about 0.800 or above) correlations with each other and when using the results of the cluster analysis, it is possible to determine that they are probably measuring the same thing, then one of the variables can be eliminated. Thus, among the demographic factors, *Population density* was eliminated in favor of *Population size* and *Population of communes* was eliminated in favor of *Percent urban*. The two social variables had similar results, so *Students* was used and *Percent literate* was not used in the refined analysis. The measures of a department's wealth, the *Number of voters in 1817 and 1831*, and the agricultural variables that measured wealth, *Agricultural revenue* and *Agricultural yield*, were eliminated in favor of *Patentes* as the number of *patentes* proves to be a good measure of wealth as well as of commercial activity. The only other variable capable of being eliminated was *Industrial production*, which was eliminated in favor of *Industrial workers*. After these refinements, 8 variables remain which effectively measure the same attributes as the original 16 variables. Now *Population size, Percent Population change, Percent Population change of communes,* and *Percent urban* measure the demographic factors; *Students* measures the social factor; and *Agricultural production, Patentes,* and *Industrial workers* measure the economic factors. *Patentes* also represents wealth.

Once these measures of the type of area each department en-

[22] Robert C. Tryon and Daniel E. Bailey, *Cluster Analysis* (New York, 1970).

compassed were refined, the object was to analyze the correlations between the SED variables and the measures of each variable on the results of the elections. A list of all the significant
correlations of the refined variables as well as the entire correlation matrix for all 16 SED variables can be found in Appendix B.

None of the SED variables correlates with an entire regime's
elections, although there is a pattern to the results of the correlations. The *Student* factor comes the closest to uniformity, as
it correlates negatively with the Right in all elections of the Restoration except for the elections of 1817–1819, 1820, and 1824.
This means that the fewer the number of students there were in
a department, the greater the percent of Right deputies there
were in that department. *Students* correlates significantly in
the positive direction with the Left in the same elections in which
the Right has the significant negative correlations, except in
1816 when the significant positive correlation is with the Center
and not the Left. Thus the Restoration begins with an attraction
between the educated areas and moderation, since both the Left
in 1815 and the Center in 1816 are moderate, whereas the Left
after 1815 is more radical. Neither the Left with its dramatic victories in 1817–1819 nor the Center with its lower success contin-
ues the relations with the socially advanced areas, but the significant positive correlation reappears in 1821–1822 with the Left.
Even though it is absent in 1824, this relationship returns in 1827
and 1830. The positive relationship between *Students* and the
Left is considerably stronger than the negative one between *Students* and the Right, thus indicating a stronger relationship between education levels of the populace and the favoring of the
Left than between ignorance of the populace and the electorate
favoring the Right. There are no significant correlations with the
social variables and the election results of the two elections of
the July Monarchy. Education is one measure of progress, and
what is clear here is that the correlation is broken after the Revolution of 1830.

The *Student* factor is the only variable with significant correlations until the elections of 1821–1822, when a new pattern
of relationships begins: *Patentes* has a significant positive correlation with the Left and a negative one with the Right. These
relationships are continued in the elections of 1824, 1827, and

1830, and in all of these later elections all four of the variables that were eliminated in favor of *Patentes* also have significant positive correlations with the Left and negative ones with the Right. Thus in 1821–1830 the areas of greater commercial activity favored the Left or, conversely, the areas of lower commercial activity favored the Right, and in 1824 yet another attribute of progress in modern societies, wealth, favored the Left, since the four eliminated variables were all measures of wealth. In addition, the level of the correlation with *Patentes* greatly increased in 1824 and reached its peak in 1827 at 0.463. This was the highest correlation between a SED variable and a party, and the 0.402 between the Left and *Patentes* in 1830 was the only other one over 0.400.

The idea that there was a connection between the progressive areas and the Left in the latter years of the Restoration is enhanced by the significant positive correlations for *Industrial production* and *Population of communes* and the Left in 1827, and *Industrial workers* and *Industrial production* and the Left in 1830. It will be recalled that these latter variables are intended to measure future change. Thus in four important ways— education, business activity, wealth, and change—there is a positive relationship between progress and the favoring of the Left in the late Restoration. The reverse is also true, but with slightly lower figures for all variables that drop the *Industrial production, Industrial workers*, and *Population of communes* below the significant level. During the 1820s a shift appears to have taken place and these relationships are all ended by the Revolution of 1830; no SED variable has a significant correlation with the parties of the July Monarchy.

The cluster analysis further elucidates the two turning points of 1821–1822 and 1830. It was performed to see if any of the variables would cluster together so that a more general description of the factors underlying the elections could be made. Clustering was done on both the 16 and the 8 groups of SED variables and on the election results. The outcome is identical. On the analysis, when only the eight SED variables are used, *Population size, Patentes*, and *Industrial workers* form a cluster with the results of 1824. This cluster has significant factor correlations (the correlation coefficient between the mean correlation of the members of the cluster and another variable) with the results of

1821–1822, 1824, 1827, and 1830. Clustering when the 16 SED variables are used reveals a cluster that includes *Patentes* and *Population size* of the previous clustering plus the 5 SED variables that have been eliminated in favor of *Patentes* and *Population size*, and *Industrial production*, which was eliminated in favor of *Industrial workers*. The election of 1824 is not in the larger cluster, but this larger cluster correlates with the election results in the same pattern as the smaller cluster.[23]

The smaller cluster represents not only population size and commercial activity but wealth too. The category of *Industrial workers* represents change and this cluster correlates at quite significant levels with the two other variables that measure change, *Percent population change* and *Percent urban*. In all cases the greater the wealth or change, the more heavily an area voted for the Left between 1821 and 1830.

The SED variables are used to discover any relationship between this type of factor and political opinion. The departments at the top and bottom of the range for each variable do not have contiguous geographic locations (see maps 1–3 for the three variables of the refined cluster). "Dynamic" North and "static" South give only a rough description of the results. In order to see if there is any geographic regionalism involved in the election results, the departments were grouped into regions. This grouping of the departments into regions was done on the basis of the traditional provinces of France, but since many of these provinces were small and because the creation of the departments often had cut across the old provincial boundaries, the regions only approximate the old provinces. Ultimately 13 regions were formed (see map 4). The regions do not lend themselves to correlation analysis, but the results of the elections are reported as the percentage for each party for each region and these figures can be examined to see if there is any regional pattern to the election results.[24]

There is a regional pattern under the Restoration which does

23 The object of calculating both clusters is to show that the inclusion of the election of 1824 in the smaller cluster did not alter the basic relationships between the cluster and the election results. See Appendix B, table 3 for the factor coefficients for both clusters and the election results.

24 See Appendix C.

□□□ Top 10 departments
▦ Bottom 10 departments

Map 1.   Population size.

not carry over into the July Monarchy. Although there are variations from election to election, and these are discussed in the later chapters, generally the northern third of the country, with the exception of the North region, favors the Left under the Restoration and the southern third of the country favors the Right. The three regions that have the highest percentage of Left deputies for the entire Restoration are Champagne, East, and Paris Area, and the three areas of least support for the Left are Aquitaine, South, and South Coast. After the Revolution of

Map 2.   Number of *patentes.*

1830 the pattern changes, since the regional distribution of the
parties is unstable in 1831 and 1834.[25]

Throughout the following chapters this material is referred
to, but two general conclusions about the data on the type of departments that the deputies represented must be emphasized.
First, there is a definite regionalism at work during the Restoration, which ends with the Revolution of 1830. Second, there is

[25] For an extension of the correlation and regional analysis to 1848 see
my forthcoming essay "The Failure of the Restoration: A Quantitative
Approach" in *1830 and the Origins of the Social Question in France,* edited
by John Merriman, New York: Franklin Watts, due 1974.

Top 10 departments
Bottom 10 departments

Map 3.   Number of industrial workers.

an undercurrent of factors which helps explain the shift in the opinion in this period. In the early 1820s there is a shift in the type of areas that support each party; this change becomes clear in 1824 when the Left wins only a handful of seats, and this new relationship remains as the Left increases its popularity. Again, the Revolution of 1830 destroys the relationship. The wealthier and more progressive areas of France have moved behind the Left by 1824 and, after remaining there for six years, these types of areas do not discriminate between the parties of the early July Monarchy. The full importance of these facts becomes clear as I analyze the characteristics of the deputies in each period.

Map 4.   Regions of France.

IV

THE NAPOLEONIC PERIOD

The coup d'état of the Eighteenth of Brumaire brought Napoleon Bonaparte to power. His position as First Consul was quickly legitimized in the new Constitution of An VIII (1800), which was written for the most part by his fellow conspirators, especially the Abbé Sieyès.[1] It created a tricameral legislature of which the lower house, the Corps Législatif, was to be elected by indirect universal male suffrage. Since the electoral laws took time to be implemented, the top legislative body, the Senate, appointed the members of the first Corps Législatif. The Corps was composed of 300 men, who held office for five years and were paid 10,000 francs per year. Renewal was to be by annual elections, wherein one-fifth of the membership would be replaced.

When the first renewal occurred in 1801 the electoral lists were not ready, so the First Consul, who had already become the dominant force in the new government, not only decided which one-fifth of the Corps should be replaced—his critics for the most part—but he also was instrumental in choosing their replacements.[2] After the Peace of Amiens and the Concordat with Rome, Bonaparte further consolidated his power in the Constitution of An X (1802), whose electoral provisions regulated all the elections of the Napoleonic period.

The Constitution of 1802 provided for elections at four levels. At the lowest level, the canton, all males who were at least 21 years old and domiciled in the canton for one year voted for elec-

---

[1] Jacques Godechot, *Les institutions de la France*, (Paris, 1968), p. 554.
[2] Ibid., p. 568.

tors. Each canton had 1 elector for every 500 inhabitants with a minimum of 120 electors and a maximum of 200 for any one canton. The canton electors then elected departmental electors, who were required to be on the list of the department's 600 highest taxed persons. This was the introduction of a censitaire system of suffrage, which derived its name from the name of the direct taxes, the *cens*. Each department had 1 elector for every 1,000 inhabitants with a minimum of 200 and a maximum of 300 electors for any one department. The departmental electoral college then chose 2 candidates for each of its department's seats to the Corps Législatif. There were no specific qualifications to be eligible for office except to be at least 30 years old and to appear on the national list of electors. The Senate, which by 1803 was subservient to the First Consul, made the final selection from the department's list of candidates.

The right to make the final choice of the members of the Corps, which he exercised through his control of the Senate, was not the only power the First Consul had over the selection of the deputies. He had the right to appoint the president of the electoral colleges, and he could add 10 men to each list of canton electors and 20 men from the top 30 tax payers of a department to each list of departmental electors.

This four-tiered system of choosing the deputies remained in force until 1814 with only three changes. In the new Constitution of 1804 Napoleon furthered his control of the elections by increasing the number of men he could appoint to the electoral lists to 25 for the canton lists and 30 for the departmental lists. Thus, after 1804 Napoleon not only controlled the appointment of the deputies but he also chose a minimum of 10 percent of the electors who chose the candidates. In 1807 the minimum age for the deputies was raised to 40 years and the deputies were made re-eligible for office. Finally, in 1811, the holding of a judicial post and being a deputy were no longer incompatible.

The annual one-fifth renewal elections began in 1803 with the new deputies beginning their terms in the session of 1804. The departments were divided into five groups with one group holding elections each year. The number of seats were apportioned to the departments by their population size and direct taxes paid. The first five elections were conducted according to the laws, but after 1808 the interference first of military victory and then of defeat prevented the smooth functioning of the electoral system. There were no elections in 1810, 1812, and 1814.

In trying to study the deputies of the Corps Législatif this lack of regard for the electoral laws creates certain problems. I found that the terms of office were not strictly observed, and therefore it was difficult to know when a man stopped serving in the Corps. In order to circumvent this problem, I grouped the deputies by the year they entered the Corps. This meant that an individual was included in my study only once no matter how long he served, unless he served in noncontiguous terms, and then he was included at each point he began a term.

The Corps Législatif was not a politically powerful institution. It had the power to reject a proposed law, but the initiative belonged to the Senate and the right to debate the proposals belonged to the middle legislative body, the Tribunat. Even this power of the Corps was gradually reduced, first in the elimination of the First Consul's critics in 1801 and subsequently in his elevation to Consul for life and then to Emperor. Napoleon never concerned himself greatly with the Corps but he did maintain it in existence, although in 1807 he abolished the Tribunat. Only in 1813, when events were proving disastrous for France, did the deputies venture an independent opinion, and then Napoleon sent them home. The Corps Législatif was primarily a showcase for Napoleon and it is in this light that I am studying its membership.

The initial members of the Corps Législatif were not dependent on the desires of Bonaparte like those chosen under the Empire, but the original members do show what type of men helped put Bonaparte in power. By studying the original group of deputies and comparing them with those eliminated in 1801 and those who were still sitting in 1803, we can more readily establish the social basis of Napoleon's early rule. What type of men he inherited from the initial Corps and how much he had modified them by the time the election of candidates began in 1803 both become apparent.

The initial Corps Législatif was dominated by men of the Revolution. Thirteen percent had sat in the Estates-General and 25 percent had participated in the Convention. Only 8 percent of the original members had not been elected to one of the revolutionary assemblies. Besides being experienced legislators, 72 percent of the deputies had held another government post during the Revolution. Their experience and also their occupations were primarily in the legal professions and government administration. Thirty percent had held positions in the magistrature; 39 percent were in the Law and 18 percent in the Government categories of Occupation. Only 6 percent were in the Military category, and I found evidence of only 2 percent who participated in the revolutionary armies.

The social class of the deputies of the initial Corps also reflected the revolutionary experience. Only three deputies were from the Titled nobility and seven more were from the Nontitled nobility; these men did not necessarily use their titles in 1800, but I found that to be their actual classification. The Bourgeois category dominated with 68 percent. These were the men who had neither noble status nor were they or their fathers close to achieving it. The Revolution had been their liberating experience.

Both their age and their experience outside the Revolution support the idea that the deputies of the initial Corps were products of the Revolution. There were few old men; only 8 percent were at least 60 years old, the smallest percentage in this category of any group in this study. Also there were a large number of young men, even for the initial legislature of a regime, which I found to be habitually overweighted with young deputies. In 1800, 17 percent were under 40 and an additional 39 percent were in their forties. Furthermore, just 17 percent of the deputies had held a post during the Old Regime.

Besides showing a close relationship to the Revolution, these initial legislators had a low involvement in the rewards of the Napoleonic period. They may have been in the original Corps, but only 27 percent would hold a post outside the Corps, only 17 percent would be awarded the Legion of Honor, and just 10 percent would be awarded an Imperial title. This lack of benefits was not due to the presence of the men who incurred Bonaparte's displeasure and were eliminated in 1801. If these men are eliminated from the initial group, still only 24 percent would earn the Legion of Honor.

Bonaparte had little control over the choosing of these initial members, but when he had consolidated his position he was able to eliminate his severest critics in the first annual one-fifth renewal in 1801. Those eliminated, however, did not show any fundamental differences from the initial members in the characteristics I measured. The eliminated group had the same age distribution, only a slightly higher percentage of Bourgeois, a few less men in the Military occupation category, and a few more men who began their legislative careers before 1795. Thus, nothing can be learned just from the characteristics of the men eliminated in 1801 which was not evident in the complete initial group, since those eliminated were chosen for the particular attribute of too great a belief in their freedom to oppose the First Consul rather than for any other characteristic. Doubtless the lack of differences in the characteristics studied indicates that they did not explain political behavior in this case. I am trying to discover if there were reasons behind men's behavior of which they were not fully aware; in this instance there are not. I am aware that there are alternatives to my characteristics as determinants of political behavior, and in this case alternatives were at work.

By 1803 the Corps Législatif was no longer primarily composed of men chosen without the approval of the First Consul. Those entering in 1802 and 1803 had been chosen by the Senate, now firmly under the control of Bonaparte, without the benefit of popularly elected candidates.

The characteristics of the deputies who were in the Corps in 1803 showed a movement away from the Revolution. There was no change in age distribution, but the Social class distribution had a greater percentage of Old Regime nobles, 7 percent. More significant for the total membership was the decline in the Bourgeois to 56 percent compared to 68 percent in the original group. Law had been the occupation most closely associated with the Revolution; its share of the deputies fell to 30 percent as the Military category increased to 11 percent. The military man who served in the Corps usually did so because his health or age rendered him unfit for combat, and thus after the initial Corps this category stabilized at about 10 percent.

It is in the areas of Experience that the change between those who began the Corps Législatif and those who were in the 1803 Corps is most readily apparent. The 1803 group had 39 percent whose appointment to the Corps began their legislative careers.

This increase in novice legislators was accomplished at the expense of those who began their careers before 1795. This group fell to 24 percent from 38 percent in the original group. Non-legislative experience of the Revolution did not wane as quickly as 65 percent of the 1803 group had held a post during the Revolution.

There was, therefore, a slight movement away from the Revolution, but a more significant movement was one toward the Napoleonic regime. Those holding a post outside the Corps rose to 55 percent from the 27 percent of the original group. It should not surprise us that the men who maintained the favor of Bonaparte were duly rewarded. This also was shown in the honors awarded. The initial deputies had only 17 percent who would win the Legion of Honor, whereas those who remained in 1803 had 34 percent win this award. The Legion of Honor was a reward for loyal support as shown by the few, 11 percent, of those eliminated in 1801 who ever managed to be awarded it. Finally, 20 percent of the men remaining in 1803 would become Imperial nobles.

The deputies of the Corps in 1803 demonstrated that Bonaparte was moving away from a total dependence on the revolutionary experience and toward the creation of his own cadre of followers. When he became Emperor in 1804 this evolution was accelerated. The deputies now were chosen from the list of elected candidates. Those selected from 1804 to 1814 support the thesis that Napoleon tried to blend the Old and the New France, especially after 1810, and that his loyal supporters were honored for their docility. The two groups of deputies who began serving in 1804–1810 and 1811–1814 clearly establish this evolution.

The distribution of the birthdates of the deputies of the two groups is one factor that did not change, even though a decade elapsed. The initial deputies had 1 percent born after 1769, the 1803 group had 2 percent, the 1804–1810 group had 6 percent, and the 1811–1814 group had 5 percent. This aging of the groups of deputies at the point they entered the Corps also can be seen in the percentage of deputies who were over 60 years old; these were 8, 9, 19, and 28 percent respectively. It should be recalled that the age requirement for the deputies was raised from 30 to 40 in 1807, but I believe this to be a reflection of the

Emperor's plan. Napoleon raised the age requirement at the same time he suppressed the Tribunat and made the deputies re-eligible for office. He apparently wanted to maintain the men he had or, if they were to be replaced, to have them replaced by men of the same generation. Besides, the Corps was not the position where ambitious men were beginning their careers.[3] The Corps was a showcase, and older men appeared to make better mannequins.

The birthdates of the two groups remained fairly stable, but the other characteristics displayed a marked change. These changes can be hypothetically separated into two types: those arising from Napoleon's desire to blend the Old and the New France and those arising from his rewarding of loyalty and his tying men to his regime with honors.[4] The old nobility, that is, the Titled plus the Nontitled categories, increased its share of the Corps slightly in 1804–1810 to 7 percent, but then the old nobility's share rose sharply in 1811–1814 to 15 percent (see fig. 1). The proportion of just the Titled nobility also increased from 3 percent to 10 percent. Although the total percentage involved was not very great, it clearly showed a trend toward reintegrating the elements of the Old Regime into the Empire. This was especially true of those with high visible status as indicated by the great increase of those with Old Regime titles. Another manifestation of the greater participation of the men of the Old France was the rise in the Near nobles. By 1811–1814 it was 29 percent to only 23 percent for the Bourgeois. The main concern of Napoleon appeared to be an Old Regime pedigree rather than experience of the Old Regime; those who had held a post under the monarchy remained steady at 30 percent for both groups.

Blending the old and the new also meant bringing more men of leisure into the Corps. Law had been the dominant occupation in 1800. By 1811–1814 Law was reduced to 28 percent;

---

[3] Ibid., p. 581. Also there was a general absence of the Corps deputies in the Chamber of Deputies after 1815.

[4] My evidence supports these hypotheses, but I do not claim to have discovered these on my own. *See* Godechot, *Les institutions de la France*, pp. 690–691; Georges Lefebvre, *Napoléon* (Paris, 1965), pp. 78, 394; J. J. Chevallier, *Histoire des institutions et des régimes politiques de la France moderne, 1789–1958* (Paris, 1967), p. 121.

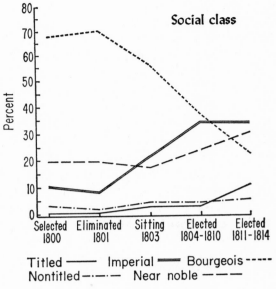

Fig. 1.   Corps Législatif.

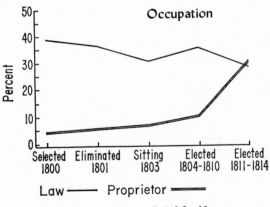

Fig. 2.   Corps Législatif.

Proprietors, however, rose to 29 percent (see fig 2). Men who had inherited their position or who had gone beyond the need to work actively for a living were being selected for the Corps. This reflected the desire to have men with higher status, but it was probably also a result of the age and the docility of the Corps. Few men of ambition were attracted to or chosen to sit in the Corps.

Less dependence was also now put on men of the Revolution, since having held a post during the Revolution no longer was so common among the deputies (see fig 3); this type of deputy declined to 47 percent in 1811–1814. Furthermore, Napoleon had ended the prohibition against émigrés. By 1811–1814, 10 percent of the deputies had managed to overcome that experience and still gain admittance to the Corps and the amount of experience of the Old Regime rose too during the Empire. The move away from the Revolution can also be seen in the dates a deputy began his legislative career (see fig. 4). New men made up over 70 percent of the two Imperial groups, since Napoleon was choosing his own men. The accompanying decline in experienced legislators was most dramatic for those men who began their careers at the height of the Revolution; those beginning before 1795 declined to 12 percent for the 1804–1810 group and to 13 percent for the 1811–1814 group. Although these figures were still fairly high, the internal composition of the experience had changed from the 1803 group. Whereas 14 percent began in the Estates-General and 16 percent in the Convention in 1803, 7 percent began in the Estates-General and only 2 percent began in the Convention in 1811–1814. Napoleon had not abandoned the deputy with an orientation toward the Revolu-

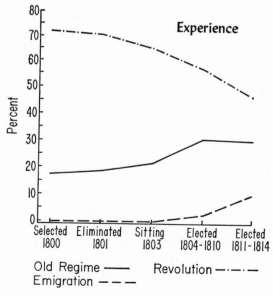

Fig. 3.   Corps Législatif.

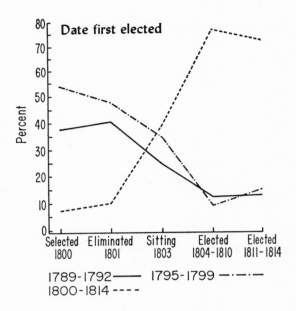

Fig. 4.   Corps Législatif.

tion, but he had mixed him with members of the traditional elites of the Old Regime.

The Marquis Etienne-Odile de Falaiseau provides a good example of the man of the Old Regime combining with the new.[5] He was born in Paris to a noble family in 1756. First coming to our attention as an émigré in 1790, he lived in Hamburg until his return to France in 1799 whereupon he soon became a principal receiver of taxes. His main occupation was that of Proprietor when, serving as the president of the college, he was selected as a candidate to the Corps Législatif from Seine-et-Marne. He was selected to serve by the Senate and he remained in the Corps from 1811 to the end of the Empire, when he accepted the return of the Bourbons and remained out of politics until his death in 1826.

Besides this clear mixture of the old and the new the post—

[5] All individuals discussed in this study were chosen after the entire text had been written, and these particular men were chosen because they illustrate my conclusions. No attempt is made to provide a random sample of illustrations.

1803 deputies also exhibited a noticeable increase in the rewards of having served Napoleon. Those who held a post outside the Corps Législatif increased to 86 percent in 1804–1810 and remained high, 77 percent, in the 1811–1814 group. More than just the rewards of office, however, were bestowed on these men. The percentage of deputies who would become Imperial nobles increased dramatically between those sitting in 1803 and the last two groups—33 percent in each of these two groups earned this distinction. Also those with the Legion of Honor rose to 49 percent in 1804–1810 and then to 58 percent in 1811–1814. The rank of the Legion of Honor also was higher in the later groups; those with a rank above the Chevalier were 12 percent in 1803, 14 percent in 1804–1810, and 26 percent in 1811–1814. Thus there were not only more honors for the later groups, but the honors were of a greater status.

The man of the Revolution as well as a new arrival could win honors under the Empire. Chevalier Gabriel-Hyacinthe Couppé de Kervennou is an illustration. Born in 1757 of a family of local officials, Couppé de Kervennou became an *avocat au parlement* at Rennes. He was a deputy for the Third Estate of the Estates-General, as secretary to the Assembly he signed the Constitution of 1791, and after serving in local administration he was elected to the National Convention first among the eight deputies of the department of Côtes-du-Nord. Voting against death for Louis XVI, then to suspend the sentence of death, and later signing the protest against the ouster of the Girondins, he fled Paris only to be arrested and imprisoned until the end of the Terror. He returned to the Convention and was elected by five departments to the Council of 500 where he served until 1799. He re-entered the magistrature after Brumaire and was elected to the Corps Législatif in 1804 and confirmed in 1809. Just prior to his election in 1804 he was awarded the Legion of Honor, and in 1811 at the same time he was appointed counselor to the Imperial court at Rennes he was also made a Chevalier of the Empire. The Chevalier Couppé de Kervennou lost his position at the Second Restoration and retired to his lands until his death in 1832.

The Napoleonic regime followed a clear pattern. It emerged out of the Revolution, and as Napoleon gained control he both tied the Corps Législatif to his personal rule and bought its acquiescence with honors. The type of deputies demonstrated that Napoleon was moving away from a strong devotion to the Revolution and that he was trying to create a new elite for France which excluded no part of her past. Other measures, such as the creation of the Imperial nobility, point in this same direction. The characteristics of the deputies are further proof of this trend.

Postscript: The First Restoration and the One Hundred Days

When Napoleon lost his power on the battlefield the new society still succeeded in maintaining itself. Louis XVIII granted the Charter of 1814, which guaranteed many of the benefits of the Revolution; the Corps Législatif was kept intact, only changing its name to the Chamber of Deputies. Like Napoleon, Louis XVIII realized the benefits of having certain representatives of the people in the government, especially when they had little real power. The Chamber of Deputies played only a minor role, and it proved itself powerless against the reaction and failures of the First Restoration. The new regime was found wanting; with the return of Napoleon, it collapsed; and with its collapse, the king fled.

Napoleon returned to France as her liberator, but he was no longer the master he had been under the Empire. In order to pose as the son of the Revolution he convinced Benjamin Constant to author the *Acte additionale aux constitutions de l'Empire*.[6] The great liberal reduced the powers of the Emperor, including his control over the elections.

The electoral system of 1802 was employed, but instead of having the canton electors elect only departmental electors, they now elected deputies directly. They chose a total of 368 deputies. Also instead of having the departmental colleges elect only lists of candidates from which the Senate chose the deputies, the departmental colleges now directly elected an additional 238 deputies. In order to give industry and commerce their own representatives, 23 more deputies were elected in 13 regional districts by the electors of the department where the regional capital was located. These deputies had to be selected from the Chambers of Commerce. All of the deputies themselves had to be at least 25

---

[6] Lefebvre, *Napoléon*, p. 576.

years old, were elected for 5 years, and were not paid. This act was the basis for the elections held in May 1815.

The atmosphere of the One Hundred Days was very different from that of the Empire. The One Hundred Days was a period of chaos and of renewed Jacobin activity. The old federations were formed, the revolutionary songs were sung, and many wanted to set up committees of public safety.[7] Western France was only barely under Napoleon's control in May 1815, with the royalist countryside and the revolutionary cities at odds with him. Southern France was in a state of turmoil, the fighting between the forces of the Duke and Duchess d'Angoulême and the Imperial army continued until April.[8] In northern and eastern France the threat of war was also present.

All of this disruption led to a low voter turnout in the elections of May—overall, 37 percent of the registered voters. The most extreme example occurred in the departmental college of Bouches-du-Rhône where only 13 voters, 4 percent, participated. The low participation was apparent almost everywhere. In only 1 percent of the elections did over three-fourths of the electors vote and in 20 percent of the elections less than one-fourth of the electors turned out. Despite the low turnout, there was often substantial competition: only 19 percent of the deputies won over three-fourths of the votes cast in their districts and 47 percent received 60 percent or less of the votes cast.

The type of man elected under these circumstances exhibited several unique features, but in general the basic profile was similar to the one for the deputy serving in 1803.[9] The One Hundred Days deputy was thus different from the type of man elected at the end of the Empire, and that difference was in the direction of the revolutionary experience. The men of leisure were missing in the One Hundred Days: the Near noble declined from 29 percent in 1811–1814 to 22 percent in the One Hundred Days, and Proprietors declined from 29 percent to 11 percent over the same two periods. In the One Hundred Days the Bourgeois again dominated with 53 percent, as did Law, with 34 percent, and Government, with 26 percent. The Titled nobility

[7] Ibid., pp. 574–575.

[8] Daniel P. Resnick, *The White Terror and the Political Reaction after Waterloo* (Cambridge, 1966).

[9] See table 5 in Appendix C.

were only 2 percent, and 3 percent were émigrés. Although most
of the deputies, 70 percent, were being elected for the first time,
those with previous legislative experience achieved it in the first
years of the Revolution. Nearly half of those previously elected
had been first elected before 1794. Also the percentage who held
a post under the Revolution remained high at 45 percent while
those with experience of the Old Regime declined to 13 percent.
The voter of the One Hundred Days was not accepting the blending of the old and the new that Napoleon had attempted; he was
moving back to the revolutionary experience in his choice of
men to represent him.

Two examples will help illustrate this change. Joseph-Jean
Jacotot, the son of a *marchant*, was born in 1770 in Côte-d'Or
where he studied and later became a professor of humanities.
Already known for his politics before the Revolution as he had
organized the youth of Dijon in defense of the new ideas, Jacotot
served in the Army of Nord in 1792–1794 where he fought in
Belgium before returning to Paris to handle the supply of
powder. After serving in Paris in the 1790s as a commissioner
of supply as well as the Assistant Director of the Ecole Polytech-
nique, Jacotot returned to Dijon to pursue his academic career.
He was Rector of the Academy of Dijon in 1809 and was arrested
by the Allies in 1814. In the One Hundred Days he was elected
to the Chamber where he supported the Constitution of the
Empire and Napoleon II. With the failure of this venture Jacotot
left France for Belgium where he taught scientific methods at
Louvain, then at the Ecole Normale Militaire en Belgique until
his return to France in 1830, where he lived in retirement until
his death in 1840.

Jean-Baptiste Vidal followed the career of his father as an
avocat. Born in 1764 in Basses-Pyrénées, he was in the departmental administration early in the Revolution before becoming
prosecutor to the Syndic in his home town. Vidal was elected as
a substitute to the National Convention and only took his seat
on October 5, 1793. He completed a successful mission to
Pyrénées-Orientales and was elected to the Council of 500 where
he served until 1797. He was not involved in public life until
being named Assistant Imperial Prosecutor in 1812, a post he
still held when elected to the Chamber of Representatives. After
the return of the Bourbons Vidal remained in the magistrature

where he rose to President of the Tribunal and retired in 1853.

Despite these two examples, one of the peculiarities of the One Hundred Days deputies was their low involvement in the Empire. Only 15 percent had served in the Corps Législatif and only one-third of these had actually begun their careers under Napoleon, as the others had served in the legislatures of the Revolution. The percentage of Imperial nobles was only 22 percent, and those holding the Legion of Honor just 32 percent. Those who held a government post under Napoleon made up 52 percent. All of these figures are markedly lower than those for the groups of deputies from the Empire.

The voters did not want the Napoleonic deputies; they had a great propensity for electing men that Napoleon had rejected. Seventeen percent of the deputies of the One Hundred Days had been elected candidates to the Corps Législatif, but they had not been selected to serve by the Senate. They were grasping at the opportunity for office that the return of Napoleon offered. It seems safe to assume that in such chaotic times such men might be more likely to undertake the risks of public office, for they have little to lose and everything to gain. This phenomenon might explain why more of the men elected in May 1815, 58 percent, held an additional post in the government than had held one under the Empire.

Hubert-Michele Vaillant was one such man selected by the voters although previously rejected by Napoleon. Born in 1760 of a near noble family, his father being a prosecutor in the Cour des Comptes, Vaillant became an *avocat au parlement* in 1782. He served the Old Regime as a receiver in the Chancellory of the Parlement of Dijon until its abolition in 1790 when he became secretary-general of the department, a post confirmed in 1800 which he held until the Second Restoration. He was twice elected by Côte-d'Or to be a candidate for the Corps Législatif, in 1804 and 1810, but never selected to sit. There was no such procedure necessary in the One Hundred Days when he was elected as a deputy. Afterwards he continued his profession as an *avocat* until his death in 1823.

The age of the deputies of the One Hundred Days was also unusual for the initial election of a regime. The One Hundred Days could qualify as an initial election as well as a last election for a regime, since it was supposed to be the new beginning ex-

pressed by Benjamin Constant and, in actuality, it proved to be
the end for Napoleon. In all the other first elections of regimes
in this study the deputies were young. In 1800 those under 40
were more than twice as numerous as those over 60. In the One
Hundred Days there were only 13 percent who were under 40
compared to 17 percent who were over 60. Furthermore, in 1815
there were more men in their fifties than in their forties; again
this violated the usual findings for an initial election. I believe
the unique opportunity the One Hundred Days provided for the
many men who had been stifled by the Empire, and for others
who felt as men of the Revolution that this was their last opportunity, explains this situation. For the former, the Empire had
shut off their rise because they had earned the displeasure of
the government. For the latter, the dam on their freedom was
shattered by the One Hundred Days, and for an entire generation that had grown up before the Revolution it was a last opportunity for office.

The career of Chevalier Antoine-Vincent Arnault, a man of let-
ters who was born in Paris in 1766 to a bourgeois family, can help
demonstrate this. He emigrated from the time of the September
Massacres until 1796. Entering the administration in 1797, he
remained in the Ministry of Interior until being removed at the
First Restoration. Arnault had been selected to the Institute in
1799, given the Legion of Honor in 1804, and named a Chevalier of the Empire in 1809. Having lost his position at the Bourbons' initial return, he was elected to the Chamber of Representatives by Paris. It was his last chance, since he was forced to leave
France when it failed. Returning to France in 1819, he only
regained his seat in the French Academy in 1829.

As just demonstrated, the total group of deputies had a lack
of legislative experience; 70 percent were entering their first
legislature. Despite this, the change did not represent the appearance of a new generation of legislators. Just 22 percent of
these deputies had been born after 1769; even though this was
much greater than the 5 percent for the last deputies of the
Corps Législatif, it was much less than for the men elected in
August 1815. The deputies of the One Hundred Days also never
had the opportunity to establish themselves.

The One Hundred Days represents both a step backward with
the return of Napoleon and a potential step forward with the

reintroduction of the men and the ideals of the Revolution. The chaos, however, caused a polarization and the Napoleonic effort at compromise was the main victim of that polarization. With the failure of this regime, France took a step in an entirely new direction.

V

THE ESTABLISHMENT
OF THE RESTORATION

The One Hundred Days was the postscript to the rule of Napoleon. His defeat at Waterloo ended his immediate influence over France and the general chaos that had accompanied his return doomed his supporters to a state of impotence. With the invasion of the allied armies came the royalist reaction: this time there would be no compromise or forgetting. Upon Napoleon's defeat in the north, Louis XVIII returned. He accepted the Charter of 1814, but this time he called new elections for August 1815 as the Chamber of the One Hundred Days was swept aside.

Most of the nation at this time was under military occupation, and the White Terror spread throughout southern France. Both of these conditions carried through the time of the elections.[1] The king, for the moment, maintained the Duke d'Otrante, or as he is better known, Joseph Fouché, as the head of the government. The duke strove to win a victory for the moderate royalists in the elections to the Chamber of Deputies.[2]

The elections of August 1815 were conducted under the provisions of the Charter of 1814 as amended by Louis XVIII upon his second return. The Charter called for a Chamber of Deputies of 268 members, which Louis expanded to 402, and it required the deputies to be 40 years of age and pay 1000 francs in

[1] Daniel Resnick, *The White Terror* (Cambridge, 1966).

[2] Guillaume de Bertier de Sauvigny, *The Bourbon Restoration* (Philadelphia, 1966), pp. 122–123.

direct taxes per year, and the electors to be 30 years of age and pay 300 francs in direct taxes. Louis changed the age requirements to 30 years to be a deputy and 25 to vote, and he maintained the tax requirements of the Charter.

The Charter of 1814 did not specify an electoral organization. Therefore, Louis decreed the system created by the Constitution of 1802 to be in effect. This meant Louis retained the power Napoleon had of appointing the presidents of the electoral colleges and of adding 10 men to the canton colleges and 20 men to the departmental colleges. Each canton college in a department, of which there were usually about four, selected a full slate of candidates for its department, and then the departmental college, whose membership was limited to between 200 and 300 electors, had to choose at least one-half of the department's deputies from these lists of candidates. Thus the cantons had a small role since the departmental colleges elected the actual deputies.

The departmental electorate for all of France numbered 20,-974 in August 1815, which was almost identical to the departmental electorate of May of 20,431. However 15,340 of this electorate voted in August compared to 7,538 in May. This did not indicate that twice as many people voted in August as in May, because there were still the canton colleges and these had elected over half the deputies in May. In both elections the number of eligible voters in the canton colleges was 72,199; in May 32,538 men elected deputies, but in August 48,478 elected only candidates.[3] Thus the two elections of 1815 were conducted with somewhat different electorates and with vastly different results.

There has been some confusion as to the effects of the voter turnout in these two elections. Bertier de Sauvigny used the percent who voted as one explanation of the change in results between the two elections, but he misused the facts.[4] He claimed seven times more people voted in August than in May, because he compared those who voted at the departmental level in May with those who voted at the canton level in August. Actually, at the canton level there were 50 percent more voters in August and at the departmental level there were 100 percent more in August. When this total voter participation is analyzed by the

[3] *Archives nationales*, FicIII (Cent Jours).
[4] Bertier de Sauvigny, *The Bourbon Restoration*, pp. 121–122.

individual elections, in May 73 percent of the deputies, regardless of which type of district elected them, were elected where
less than half the voters turned out, and in August only 7 percent
were in this category. Although the August elections did not
have the very low turnout of May, neither did they have very
much high participation, since only 25 percent of the deputies
were elected where participation was over three-quarters of the
registered voters. The abstentions were much greater in May,
but they were nevertheless significant in August as well.

What cannot be known is what type of man abstained in the
two elections. It seems reasonable to assume that the May voter
saw something positive in Napoleon's return. Many of the royalist leaders were in exile and in small constituencies this could
have been critical in the decision of others not to vote. Many
royalists also refused to swear to the new constitution which
denied them the vote.[5] In August, on the other hand, the royalist
terrorism would have discouraged liberal voters, and doubtless
there would be a tendency for those who had been in the public
spotlight to seek shelter. It seems probable that the clear differences between May and August were caused in part by the
select voting, but contrary to the interpretation of Bertier de
Sauvigny they were not a product of mass abstentions.

The deputies elected in May did not represent a new generation; the deputies elected in August did represent a new generation, and this new generation was distinguished not only by a
difference in age but by a new type of man. The deputies of
the Second Restoration were not bourgeois; they were dominated
by the traditional elites. The Old Regime Titled nobles comprised 36 percent of the deputies, Nontitled 9 percent, and Near
nobles 28 percent, leaving only 15 percent Bourgeois. The occupational categories also reflected the change. Law declined
from 34 percent in May to 12 percent in August; Proprietors rose
from 11 percent to 39 percent.

Besides having different social backgrounds, the men of the
Second Restoration, on the average, were younger than the men
of the One Hundred Days. In August there were more men
under 40 than over 60, and more in their forties than in their
fifties. In terms of their birthdates, 22 percent elected in May

[5] Marquise de Montcalm, *Mon journal, 1815–1818, pendant le premier
ministère de mon frère* (Paris, 1936), p. 25.

had been born after 1769 to 33 percent in August. For the first time there were also more deputies born after 1769 than before 1760. This indicates that the men who led the reaction were not just men who wanted to return to the good old days where they had enjoyed the benefits of the Old Regime. These were the first generation of men who had been denied the benefits of the Old Regime and perhaps this accounts for their passionate and reactionary views. The youthfulness of these men also helped them persist throughout the Restoration.

The first generation of the Second Restoration was composed almost completely of different individuals from those elected in May, or for that matter in the Empire also. In August 80 percent of the deputies were being elected to their first legislature; only 5 percent had been elected in May and only 10 percent had served in the Corps Législatif. Thus in the space of one year there were in terms of personnel three virtually independent legislatures.

The previous experience of the two groups elected in 1815 showed the total reversal that occurred among the voting electorate. The One Hundred Days deputies included only 13 percent who had held a post during the Old Regime and 3 percent who had been émigrés; the Second Restoration deputies included 23 percent who had held a post during the Old Regime and 21 percent who had been émigrés. The positive attitude toward the Revolution in May produced 45 percent who had held a post during that period; the reaction against it produced deputies of whom only 20 percent had held a post during the Revolution. Also 11 percent of the men of May had fought in the armies of the Revolution; among the men of August 11 percent had fought in the armies that opposed the Revolution. There were also 38 men elected in May who had voted on the fate of Louis XVI; 20 of these had voted his death. In August only 5 had voted, 2 for death.[6] Twenty-five of the men of May had sat in the Constituent

---

[6] In this study I was concerned with who was elected; therefore if a man was elected in more than one department he was included each time he was elected. He was also included whether he actually took his seat or not. In this particular case Fouché, a regicide, was elected in two departments but he never took his seat. If I had studied only those who participated in the Chamber, the count here would have been three members of the Convention with none voting for death. In the entire study there were only 128 multiple elections, and it was rare for a man not to take his seat.

Assembly, 22 of them in the Third Estate; 13 men of August had sat then, only 6 in the Third Estate. Lastly, 108 of the men of May had sat in the Councils of the Directory, only 23 men of August had.

The deputies of August 1815 had another notable difference in their experience—there was a sharp increase in military men who won election. As I discussed previously, there were few men in the Military category in the Corps Législatif and in the Chamber of the One Hundred Days. In August there were more in the Military, 16 percent, than in any other Chamber analyzed in this study. These men usually had no connection with the Republican or Imperial armies, but instead they were associated with the old royal army. Usually they had been in the army under the Old Regime, had emigrated and often fought against the Revolution, and then were reintegrated into the French army upon the return of Louis XVIII in 1814. By 1815 many of these men had not been active in military affairs since 1795; after reclaiming their positions in the military in 1814 they usually retired soon thereafter. This body of men sat on the Right, and it is the characteristics of this group of deputies which one thinks of when the Chamber of 1815 is called the Chambre Introuvable.

The Count Louis-Charles de Vogué and the Marquis Georges-Léonard de Tramecourt were two such deputies. Count de Vogué was of the old nobility. Born in 1769 in Gard, he had emigrated in 1792 with his family; returning only when the Bourbons did, he was made a Brigadier-General. During the One Hundred Days he joined the army of the Duke d'Angoulême. A man of great wealth, whose taxes were 13,800 francs in 1820, he was elected to the Chamber of Deputies from Gard. He sat with the majority and was re-elected in 1816, 1820, and 1822 before being named a Peer in 1823. The Marquis de Tramecourt was also an émigré, but he returned in 1800, after having fought with the Duke de Condé. He had been born in 1766 in Pas-de-Calais and was in the Royal army from 1782 until the Revolution, but his title stemmed only from the First Restoration. During the Empire he had served on the Council General of his department as he was again to do in 1824. The Marquis was re-elected only in 1820, and he maintained his representation of Pas-de-Calais until he was raised to the Chamber of Peers in 1827. Like de Vogué, de Tramecourt was in the majority in 1815 and supported the Right in his entire career.

The large amount of military experience of the deputies of the Second Restoration was not the only experience they had in the government, as can be seen in the career of the Marquis de Tramecourt. Other historians have claimed that the Chambre Introuvable was composed of men without knowledge of the New France.[7] This, I believe, is assumed because of the presence of so many émigrés and the overall lack of legislative experience.[8] These correct facts were readily available to both contemporaries and historians, and therefore they have been utilized. I have found in my study, however, that in addition to the émigrés there were 20 percent of the deputies who had held a post during the Revolution and 46 percent who had held a post during the Empire. The Napoleonic office-holders are particularly significant. If military experience was excluded, 40 percent of the deputies had still served in the Imperial government. By way of comparison, there were 43 percent with similar experience elected in May. Much of this experience was at the local level, as in the career of Joseph-André de Lauro, who was vice-mayor from 1807 to 1813 and mayor from 1813 to 1827. A proprietor by occupation de Lauro was one of the young men of the Right, having been born in 1778, who would support the Right throughout the Restoration. Because of the new electoral laws de Lauro was too young to run for re-election in 1816, but he was re-elected in 1820 and served until the Revolution of 1830. Another such deputy with local experience was François-Mathieu Dahirel, an *avocat*, who served as a tax collector from 1801 and was elected by Morbihan as an Ultra in August 1815. The large

[7] S. Charléty, *La Restauration* (Paris, 1921), p. 91; Bertier de Sauvigny, *The Bourbon Restoration*, p. 130; René Rémond, *The Right Wing in France from 1815 to DeGaulle* (Philadelphia, 1966), pp. 39–40.

[8] Bertier de Sauvigny plays down the importance of the émigrés, because he claims most held positions under the Empire. I disagree because in the total study only about 10 percent of the deputies who were émigrés held a post during the Napoleonic period. I also have found that none of the émigrés in this study held a post during the Revolution. Although this may seem obvious, the years 1789–1791 were included in the Revolution period and it is this early period of the Revolution and the latter years of the Empire when men without any commitment to the New France may have held a post.

number of deputies of the Second Restoration like de Lauro and Dahirel with personal knowledge of the New France should not be overlooked in trying to explain their reaction. With this much experience I believe it is incorrect to characterize the acts of the Chambre Introuvable as being caused by ignorance of France.

Another misconception about the men of the Second Restoration concerns the amount of status they possessed. Status or prestige is a difficult concept to evaluate, but I think there are certain outward manifestations that can be examined. I have used the possession of either the Legion of Honor or the Order of Saint Louis and also whether a man was among the Titled nobility to measure status. Of course it is possible, and in the case of the opponents of the government probable, that I have underestimated the amount of status, since a man could have great status and not hold one of these honors or titles. However, I feel the reverse is much less probable.

In the Second Restoration, 43 percent of the deputies held the Legion of Honor and 31 percent held the Order of Saint Louis, so that 60 percent had at least one of the two. This was nearly twice as many as in May. Forty-eight percent of the Chambre Introuvable also had either an Old Regime or Imperial title. The *hoberaux* noble was not a significant portion since there were four times as many noble deputies with Old Regime titles as those without titles. Lastly, the amount of direct taxes paid by these deputies, which provides an approximation of a man's wealth, was consistent with later legislatures of the Restoration and considerably greater than for the men elected in May. In May, 45 percent had paid over 1,500 francs in direct taxes; in August, 64 percent had paid over 1,500 francs. Thus the men of the Chambre Introuvable were not *hoberaux*; many were men of status.

So far I have been discussing the total membership of the Chamber of Deputies. Beginning with the Second Restoration, however, the Chamber had a significant amount of political power. Although there was no strict adherence to the concept of ministerial responsibility, since in fact this question was a main concern of the politics of the Chambre Introuvable, the majority in the Chamber could no longer be ignored. In 1813 Napoleon simply sent home the Corps Législatif when it displeased him. During the Restoration Louis XVIII could dissolve the Chamber, but he immediately had to call new elections. The new presence of political power in the Chamber gave rise to the formation of groups, more or less organized, which shared political opinions.

In the Chambre Introuvable these groups were just two in number: the Ultras, or as I will call them the Right, who were led from outside the Chamber by the Count d'Artois, and the Left, or Ministerial Minority, who supported the king and the government of the Duke de Richelieu. The Right won an overwhelming majority, 78 percent, in August, and its members had a markedly different profile from the deputies who supported the government.

There was no variation in the ages or in the taxes paid of the Right and Left, but there was a difference in their social backgrounds and experience. The Right was dominated by the traditional elites: 42 percent were Titled nobles of the Old Regime, 10 percent were Nontitled nobles, and only 12 percent were Bourgeois. Forty-one percent of the Right were Proprietors, 22 percent were Military, and only 10 percent were Law. The Left group was closer in type to the men who had served Napoleon: 33 percent were Imperial nobles, 25 percent were Bourgeois, and only 16 percent were Titled nobles. Only 15 percent were Proprietors to 19 percent Law and 34 percent Government (see figs. 5 and 6).

More than just outward social aspects of the deputies, however,

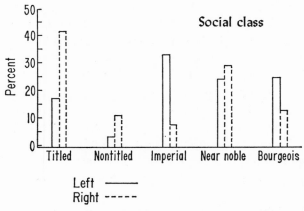

Fig. 5.   Chambre Introuvable.

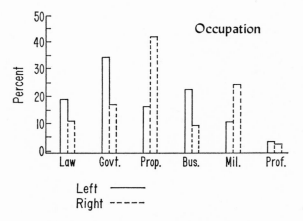

Fig. 6.   Chambre Introuvable.

separated the two groups. As one would expect, the Right had little experience with the Revolution but great experience in opposition to the New France. Only 10 percent of the Right had served in a previous legislature; none had served in the One Hundred Days. On the Right, fewer men, 20 percent, had held a post during the Revolution than had been émigrés, 24 percent. Thirty-eight percent had served Napoleon, but during the crucial period of the One Hundred Days only 2 percent supported Napoleon to 22 percent who opposed his return. Twenty-three men actually emigrated in early 1815 and still managed to return and win election in August.

The Left group exhibited a more positive attitude toward the Revolution and manifested an especially strong preference for the Imperial period. Thirty-four percent of the Left had held a post during the Revolution and just 7 percent had been émigrés; 74 percent had held a post under Napoleon. Also, 16 percent had begun their legislative careers in a revolutionary assembly, 14 percent in the Corp Législatif, and 14 percent in May 1815. The One Hundred Days was more divisive for the Left, when 18 percent supported Napoleon and 25 percent opposed him. The large percent who did not support the return of Napoleon indicated the strong reaction against the atmosphere of the One Hundred Days, but this should not obscure the basic commitment to the Imperial regime that had been present.

A final difference between the two groups concerns the area

of France their members represented. Whereas only *Students* of the SED variables had a significant correlation, —0.259 with the Right, the regional pattern of the Restoration was apparent. Even though the Right dominated in nearly every region of France, it did particularly well in the South, Aquitaine, Channel, North, Center, and Mountain regions. It did poorest in the East, Champagne, and Lower West regions.

There have been many explanations for the Right's success and the geographical distribution of that success can help evaluate these explanations. Besides the general conservative movement of August 1815, two specific causes of the success of the Right have been advanced: the presence of the *Chevaliers de la foi* and the White Terror.[9] The *Chevaliers de la foi* was an organization of men, mostly nobles, who had a strong belief in the need to restore and maintain the monarchy. They had first organized clandestinely in 1813. In 1814 this group was important in creating the impression that the Bourbons were popular in France by organizing public demonstrations in support of the return of Louis XVIII. The organization was going to maintain itself into the 1820s as a solid force of Ultra opinion. The White Terror, on the other hand, was the retribution against those who supported Napoleon's return by the supporters of the Bourbons. Both, of course, were part of the reaction of 1815, but the question here is what were their specific influences on the elections? In the case of the *Chevaliers de la foi*, where it was strong it did not uniformly coincide with a strong vote for the Right (see map 5). The Lower West was one of several strongholds of the *Chevaliers de la foi*, but its percentage of Right deputies was only 68 percent, which was well below the national average of 78 percent (see map 6).[10] The *Chevaliers de la foi* was also a continuing movement and many areas where it was strong, as in the North, supported the Right in 1816 at or below the national average (see map 7).[11] That is, the *Chevaliers de la foi* could not hold the voters once the conditions of 1815 had passed, which leads to the conclusion that it was probably not the cause of the devotion of the North to the Right in 1815. The *Chevaliers de la foi* was also strong in Aquitaine and Provence,

[9] Bertier de Sauvigny, *The Bourbon Restoration*, pp. 13–15, 122.
[10] And see percentages in table 7, Appendix C.
[11] And see percentages in table 7, Appendix C.

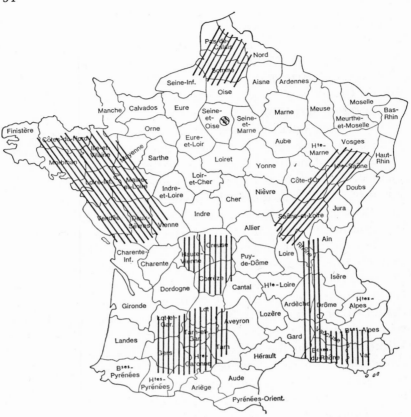

Map 5.   Strongholds of the *Chevalier de la foi* in 1815
(from Bertier de Sauvigny, pp. 13–15).

but here and in certain other areas of the Midi the presence of
the *Chevaliers de la foi* coincided with the eruption of the White
Terror.

There was a strong relationship between those areas that experienced the White Terror and a strong vote for the Right. The
entire southern third of France was involved. I believe, however, that the White Terror was not the cause of the heavy vote
for the Right because this same area was going to show a strong
preference for the Right throughout the Restoration, and the
White Terror ended in 1816. Thus neither the *Chevaliers de
la foi* nor the White Terror appear to have been the cause of the
great success of the Right; all three seem to have been symptoms
of the reaction of the Second Restoration.

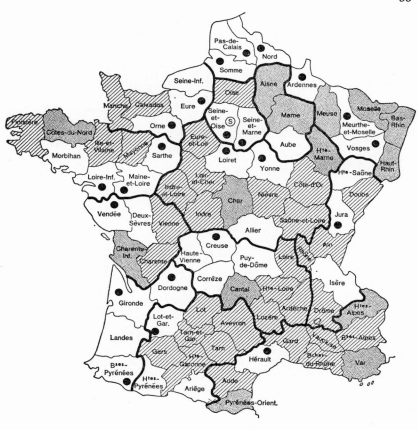

100 percent Right deputies*

50 percent and over Left deputies

* The departments marked with a dot were in the 75 percent and over Right deputies category, but since the Right won such a large percentage of the seats only those departments with 100 percent Right deputies are marked on the map.

Map 6. Elections of August 1815, by department.

Examining the areas that voted for the Left in August 1815 also does not clarify any specific explanation for the results of the voting. The East was one area that voted for the Left, and this may appear to have been an influence of the war. The Allies had occupied this area and a fear of the Allies may have provided a patriotic reaction.[12] However, there were 61 departments that

[12] Paul Leuilliot, *L'Alsace au début du XIXe siècle* (Paris, 1959), 1:153–167. Leuilliot believes the occupation definitely helped the Left.

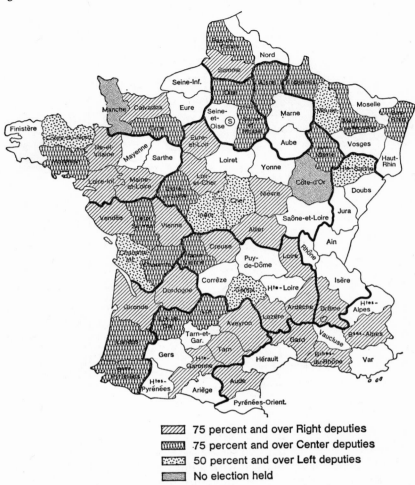

75 percent and over Right deputies
.75 percent and over Center deputies
50 percent and over Left deputies
No election held

Map 7.   Elections of 1816, by department.

were occupied during the elections and they did not show any
consistency in the group they favored in the election.[13] Also,
proximity to the battle zones did not appear to exert an influence
either—the department of Nord elected 10 of 12 and that of
Ardennes 4 of 5 Right deputies.

[13] Jean Vidalenc, *Le département de l'Eure sous la monarchie constitutionnelle, 1814–1848* (Paris, 1952), pp. 85–87. Vidalenc feels the occupation
had no effect.

What occurred in August was a general reaction against the revolutionary tradition and also a reflection of a basic geographical split in France. The One Hundred Days had brought back memories of the chaos of 1793. The reaction to these events took place throughout the country, but the intensity was due to a regional tradition. The South would be the bedrock of support for the Right throughout the Restoration, just as the East would remain firmly committed to the Left. The *Chevaliers de la foi*, the White Terror, and the results of the elections all seemed to arise out of a general reaction; they do not appear to have been a great influence on each other.

The overwhelming weight of the reaction against the revolutionary tradition is demonstrated in the profile of the deputies who supported the government. These men are given the label of Left in this study, but they were not men who would maintain their position on the Left. They were brought together by their opposition to the Ultras and not necessarily by the opposition to the monarchy which was to distinguish the Left in the remainder of the Restoration.[14] It becomes clear in later chapters that their experience and social composition was not as one-sided in favor of the Revolution as later Left groups. More importantly, of the 88 men on the Left in 1815, only 12 of the 58 who won re-election in 1816 continued to sit on the Left. The remaining 46 belonged to the Center group, which supported the government. Thus only between 3 and 10 percent of the deputies of the Second Restoration were actually on the Left as defined in reference to the entire Restoration.

The conservative tide in August was so strong that it even swamped the power of the government. The Ultras won 78 percent of the seats despite the efforts of the government in favor of moderate royalist candidates. Fouché used the influence of the government in what was to become a traditional manner: employing the presidents of the electoral colleges as the government's spokesmen or often even the government's candidates.

[14] Contemporaries characterized the deputies of the Chambre Introuvable as belonging to either the Ministerial Minority, the Left for my purposes, or to the Ultra majority. Unfortunately, this made it impossible to distinguish the liberals from the moderate royalists, as I will do for the elections of 1816.

Fouché, through the king, had men he believed were moderates appointed as presidents of the electoral colleges, except where a member of the royal family was appointed.[15] Of the 86 departments, 43 elected their president to the Chamber; unfortunately for Fouché and the king only 8 of these men would remain loyal to the government. The government's authority had produced meager results in face of the reaction.

The electorate, however, did not want the Old France back since it had reacted against the disorder of the revolutionary days, which many saw for themselves for the first time. Although the reaction was not ephemeral, the worst had passed by 1816. The king, being unable to work with the Ultras, dissolved the Chamber in September 1816 and took a chance that the electorate would support him in the new elections.

Because the Ultra majority and the government had been unable to reach agreement on an electoral law, the king again used his personal power to authorize the elections. He abolished the changes in the Charter he had implemented in 1815. The size of the new Chamber would thus be only 258 compared to 402 elected in August 1815, and the age requirements for deputies was returned to 40 years and for the voters to 30 years. The system of indirect suffrage was continued. The change in the age requirements mean that all those born from 1776 to 1785 were no longer eligible to be deputies. Many incumbents were thus prohibited from seeking re-election in 1816.

The country had returned to more normal conditions by the fall of 1816, even though the Allied occupation continued. The election was conducted with the government advocating the rejection of the Ultras. Elié Decaze, who ran the government's campaign, chose the presidents of the electoral colleges with the intention of furthering the government's interests.[16] This action, plus the dissolution itself, sparked bitterness among the Ultras: two departments, Côte-d'Or and Manche, could not reach a quorum for the entire election and Eure obtained a quorum only on the first day and thus elected only one of its four deputies, because the Ultras refused to participate.[17] Despite such

---

15 Bertier de Sauvigny *The Bourbon Restoration*, p. 122.
16 Ibid., p. 138.
17 Ibid. and Vidalenc, *Le département de l'Eure*, p. 185.

feelings, the government triumphed in 1816. The Center group, which supported the government, won 44 percent, and when combined with the 10 percent that the Left won the government was able to control the new Chamber. The Ultras had been reduced to 44 percent.

The calmer times and the reaction against the excesses of the Ultras were important causes of the shift in the composition of the Chamber. One factor, however, which changed very little from the August 1815 election was the voter turnout. Only 30 percent of the deputies in 1816 were elected in areas where over three-quarters of the electorate participated; this was close to the 25 percent for 1815. The Ultra abstentions resulted in no election or they were concentrated, so they did not affect these figures, and there was no clear indication in 1816 of what type of voter did not participate.

When voters did participate, there were more closely contested elections in 1816. Both the Left and the Right deputies in 1816 had a greater percentage who received less than 56 percent of the votes cast than they had in 1815. For the Left 52 percent and for the Right 38 percent had this narrow margin of victory in 1816 compared to 39 percent and 32 percent respectively in 1815. One oddity in the statistics is explained by the behavior of the Ultras; the Left had a very large percentage, 29 percent, which won over three-quarters of the votes cast and this occurred where the Left and Right combined to defeat the government.

The changes that did occur in 1816 can be seen best by examining the profiles of the men who were not re-elected in 1816 and comparing them with the men who were elected in 1816. Considering the influences of the government, the actions of the previous Chamber, and the calmer climate in the country, it is not surprising that the Right was the primary group eliminated in 1816. There were 224 men who were elected in August 1815 and not re-elected in 1816, and 85 percent of them were on the Right. Consequently, the profile of the men eliminated was very similar to the Right group of 1815.

The factors that separated the two groups were both their social background and certain aspects of their experience. Over 40 percent of those eliminated were Old Regime Titled nobility compared to only 25 percent for those elected in 1816. Unlike what may have been expected from the previous groups, the Proprietors did not decline as drastically as the Titled nobility; their overall strength fell to 30 percent in 1816 since 37 percent of those eliminated were Proprietors.

If any one type of man was eliminated in 1816, it was the deputy of the Right who had a strong connection to the royal army. In conjunction with the decrease on the Right of Titled nobles and Military men, there was also a decline of men with the Order of Saint Louis, military experience of the Old Regime, and military experience of the Second Restoration. This type of man was swept into office during the height of the reaction and this type of deputy will appear again in the election of 1824, but he could not sustain himself in the atmosphere of 1816.

There were several peculiarities in the experience of these groups. Being an émigré appeared to have no effect on one's chances of winning re-election: 21 percent in 1815, 21 percent of those eliminated, and 20 percent in 1816 were émigrés. What did occur was a relative popularity of this type of deputy for the Ultra voter: the Right in 1816 had 32 percent émigrés. If being an émigré made a man more popular with the Ultra voter, having a connection with the Empire made a man very unpopular with this voter in 1816. The Right in 1815 had 38 percent with Napoleonic experience; the Right in 1816 had only 16 percent with Napoleonic experience. The Right's disdain for Napoleonic men was not reflected in the overall figures; these men were popular on the Left and Center, so that the total membership of the Chamber actually had more Imperial nobles and men who had held a post under the Empire in 1816 than in 1815.

The only other noticeable change from 1815 to 1816 was in the success of the deputies whose occupation was Business. This category is of particular interest because of its possible relationship to the dominance of businessmen during the July Monarchy. In 1815, as consistently throughout the Napoleonic period, about 10 percent of the deputies were in this category; whereas if the Chamber in 1815 is analyzed by party, then 21 percent of the Left and only 8 percent of the Right were in the Business category. This is what the current historiography would lead one to expect, since businessmen would not favor the return to the

Old Regime.[18] In 1816 the Business deputy was very successful; overall, 18 percent of the Chamber were in this category since both the Left, 33 percent, and the Right, 15 percent, had a greater percentage of such deputies than in 1815. As these figures would indicate, few, only 5 percent, of those eliminated in 1816 were in Business. As discussed later, I believe the calmer atmosphere helped this type of man win election in 1816, and the Business category remained at about 20 percent for the remainder of the time period studied.

In trying to explain the results of 1816 by the type of department electing the deputies, one finds that the more socially backward areas favored the Right—both the *Student* and the *Percent literate* variables had significant negative correlations with the Right. The Left, on the other hand, had no significant correlations. It was the Center and not the Left as in 1815 which had a positive correlation of significance with the *Student* variable, and it was also the Center that was successful in the regions that had favored the Left in 1815. These facts indicate that the Center in 1816 and the Left in 1815 represented the same attributes.

Besides the social factors' relationship to the results of 1816, the regional pattern remained a strong influence in the distribution of the deputies. The southern and central parts of France were again loyal to the Right, but the Channel and North regions switched from support of the Right in 1815 to support of the Center in 1816. The East again supported the Left, but it gave greater support to the Center as did Champagne and the Paris Area regions. Remembering that many of the men of the Left in 1815 moved into the Center afterwards, the regional distributions of 1815 and 1816 were very similar.

In summary, what was established in 1815—1816 was the general outline of the Restoration regime. It began with a strong reaction to the One Hundred Days, but the basic outline was nevertheless set. The Right was to dominate with its dependence on the Old Regime nobility, on men with experience outside the revolutionary tradition, and on men who were elected from

---

[18] Regional studies provide conflicting evidence on the attitude of businessmen. Often one's view of the Empire also affected the situation and the Empire was identified with the Left. For example, see Leuilliot, *L'Alsace au début*, p. 310, and Vidalenc, *Le département de l'Eure*, p. 389.

the South. Its overwhelming position was undercut in 1816, but these essential features remained. The Restoration was not going to be the regime of the bourgeois, of the men in the active occupations, or of the men with a dedication to the New France. The Left opposition was to have its day, twice in fact, yet the first time would only be a hiatus in the preponderance of the Right.

VI

HIATUS: 1817-1819

The government was successful in ousting the Right in the elections of 1816 and Richelieu continued to lead the government with the support of the Center and some of the Left. However, once the danger of reaction began to fade an opposition group was created on the Left. This was a small group in 1816, but it continued to grow until 1820. In 1819 Elié Decaze took over as the chief minister of Louis XVIII and he continued to rule with a Center-Left coalition.

On the surface these were successful years for the government —the national finances were stabilized and the indemnity imposed in 1815 was paid. This allowed the allied occupation to end in 1818. The army was reorganized under the Laws of St. Cyr in the same year, thus ending the problem of combining the traditions of the Royal and Imperial armies. Finally a new electoral law was passed, which was believed to be unfavorable to the Right.[1]

The new law on elections did not tamper with the requirements set forth in the Charter; instead it replaced the electoral organization of the Constitution of 1802. The new law called for direct elections, which were to be held at only the departmental level. There no longer would be canton nominating elections; all eligible voters would vote in the departmental colleges and the elections would be held in the departmental capital. It was this last provision that the deputies believed would hurt the

[1] Frederick B. Artz, "The Electoral System in France during the Bourbon Restoration, 1815–1830," *Journal of Modern History* 1 (June 1929): 217.

Right, since it favored the urban voter, who was less likely to vote for the Right, rather than the rural voter, who would have to make the journey to the capital in order to vote.[2] The electoral colleges usually met for about a week, so the voter who did not live in the capital had to undergo a considerable expense in order to participate.

The power of the government in elections also was reduced. The king no longer could appoint additional members to the electoral colleges. He did, however, retain his right to appoint the president of the electoral colleges. Finally, the deputies would have five-year terms of office, but one-fifth of the membership would be renewed each year. Dividing the departments into five groups, the new law called for one group to hold elections each year.

The electoral law of 1817 was to be employed for only three years. Those three elections form a hiatus in the dominance of the Right during the Restoration, since there was a continuing movement toward the Left in the partial elections of 1817, 1818, and 1819. The Left won only 10 percent in 1816, then 29 percent, 53 percent, and 70 percent thereafter. The increase in the size of the Left group was won at the expense of the Right in 1817 and 1818 and at the expense of the Center in 1819. The type of man elected in 1817–1819 also changed and the increase in the Left explains many, but not all, of the new aspects of the profiles of these deputies.

The Left group, as established in the previous chapter, was oriented toward the Revolution in its experience. In 1817–1819 the Left was more involved in the Revolution than the previous Left group, since only 43 percent of the Left in 1816 had held a post during the Revolution compared to 49 percent in 1817–1819. The Right's share with this type of experience, however, declined from 17 percent in 1816 to 8 percent in 1817–1819. At least on this measure of the deputies there was a large increase in the difference between the Left and Right deputies in the elections of 1817–1819.

This trend was also evident in the experience of the One Hundred Days. While the Right continued to have virtually no

2 Georges-Denis Weil, *Les élections législatives depuis 1789* (Paris, 1895), pp. 92–93, and Louis Girard, *Le libéralisme en France de 1814 à 1848* (Paris, 1967), p. 18.

members who held a post during Napoleon's return the Left deputies with this experience increased from 29 percent in 1816 to 39 percent in 1817–1819. There were also more men who began their legislative careers during the One Hundred Days elected in 1817–1819, and the entire increase was on the Left since no deputies on the Right had begun their careers in May 1815. Opposition to the return of Napoleon declined from 1816 to 1817–1819 both on the Left, from 10 percent to 3 percent, and on the Right, from 24 percent to 13 percent. Thus the orientation toward the Revolution and its revival in the One Hundred Days was still the clear dividing line between the two groups. This was expected, but what is of consequence here is the increase in this distinction between 1816 and 1817–1819.

The other areas of experience displayed a somewhat different pattern. The experience of the Old Regime had an overall decline as the party groups became more similar. In 1816 the Left had 14 percent, the Right 26 percent; in 1817–1819 the Left had 18 percent, the Right 21 percent. The experience of the emigration showed the same pattern, but to a much smaller degree. It was, however, the Napoleonic experience that displayed the greatest amount of convergence. Those who held a post under Napoleon increased from 1816 to 1817–1819, yet unlike the experience of the Revolution and One Hundred Days the deputies of the Left with this type of experience actually declined from 76 percent to 60 percent. At the same time, the deputies on the Right with experience of the Empire rose from 16 percent to 33 percent. Finally, both groups had far fewer men who had connections to the Second Restoration, either in the government or in the legislature. The total experience of the men elected in 1817–1819 showed the Left to be favoring men with more radical backgrounds while the Right was turning to men with more moderate backgrounds.

Although the strength of the political groups cannot explain the change in the experience of the deputies elected in 1817–1819, it can explain most of the changes in the social composition of these deputies. The Old Regime Titled nobles comprised 25 percent in 1816 and only 5 percent in 1819 and the Imperial nobles comprised 18 percent in 1816 and 32 percent in 1819, but neither the Left nor the Right had a significant change in their Social class distribution. The Right did have a sharp increase in

Nontitled nobles, but this was a small group to begin with. Thus the change that can be observed in the overall shift in the Social class of the deputies in the 1817–1819 period was due to the modification in the strength of the parties.

The total group for 1817–1819 demonstrated little change in their distribution of occupations, but there were some internal shifts in the Left. There was a sharp decrease on the Left in Law, from 38 percent in 1816 to 23 percent in 1817–1819, and in Business, from 33 percent to 23 percent, and there was a large rise in the number of Proprietors, from 5 percent to 23 percent, and in Military, from zero to 10 percent. No change exists in the figures for the total group of deputies because the increase in the strength of the Left was balanced on the Right and Center by a decline in the occupational categories where the Left was usually strong and an increase where it was usually weak. This type of movement at first led me to think there might be some force that kept the occupational distribution within certain limits, but later elections show this to be untrue. The changes, therefore, must have come out of the atmosphere of these years and not some general cause.

Historians have employed the Napoleonic resurgence in these years to explain the success of the Left, but without enough precision.[3] I have already discussed how the Napoleonic experience actually declined on the Left and the increase came on the Right. A close examination of this phenomenon establishes that a few prominent Napoleonic figures did re-enter politics, which explains why more of the deputies were Imperial nobles in 1817–1819 than previously. For example, General Horace-François Sébastiani de la Porta, a soldier for France from August 1789 to 1814, a count of the Empire, and a deputy in the One Hundred Days, was elected in 1819; but what is too often ignored is that General Marie-Joseph de Lafayette, a marquis and a prominent Republican, Jacques-Antoine Manuel, an *avocat*, an avid Bonapartist, a member of the army in 1792–1796, and a deputy in May 1815, and Michael Laroche, a banker and merchant, were also elected in 1817–1819. Sébastiani and Lafayette represent the prominent men, Manuel the well-studied deputy who justifies the historian's case for the revival of Bonapartism; but what

[3] S. Charléty, *La Restauration* (Paris, 1921), pp. 112–137.

needs to be remembered is that the little-known Michel Laroche represents the bulk of the deputies elected in 1817–1819—with these deputies it was the experience of the Revolution and not Napoleon that was more noticeable.

I think the explanation for the success of the Left during these years is actually found in the return of certain individuals to the Chamber and in the general acceptance of the Restoration as a permanent regime. The One Hundred Days was a traumatic experience, which took time for the Left to overcome. By 1817, and especially by 1819, this experience had been conquered, and the men who had served in the One Hundred Days were ready to return to politics and the voter was ready to accept them. Although this involved Napoleonic figures, such as General Sébastiani, the atmosphere was actually more oriented toward the Revolution. General Lafayette had been a deputy in the One Hundred Days and then, as in 1818, he was not looking to revive the Empire; he wanted the Revolution to triumph. The voter seemed to want men of the Revolution.

Historians have often used the luminaries to describe these elections.[4] I want to turn to the total membership elected in 1819 to demonstrate the pattern that had evolved in the years of success for the Left. The election of 1819 was a great success for the Left and for the men of the Revolution. The Left's opposition to the government had become more pronounced during the Restoration and this group won a great victory in 1819 when it won 70 percent of the seats.

The profile of the men elected in 1819 reflected this dominance of the Left, but it went beyond that; these men had a more pronounced profile in favor of the Revolution and its tradition. Many of them were old, 27 percent were over 60. Only 32 percent of them were born after 1769, nearly the same percentage as in the Chambre Introuvable. For the most part, their age meant that they were of the generation that made the Revolution, and unlike many of the men elected earlier in the Restoration they had actually done much of the making. These men had not been in the revolutionary assemblies, only 14 percent had begun their legislative careers then, but 50 percent had held a

[4] G. Bertier de Sauvigny, *The Bourbon Restoration* (Philadelphia, 1966), p. 163.

post during the Revolution. This was even more than for the deputies of the One Hundred Days. Combined with the high experience of the Revolution was a low experience in the Old Regime, 13 percent, and in emigration, 4 percent. The service of the 1819 deputies to the New France was also apparent under Napoleon, 11 percent had begun their legislative careers in the Corps Législatif and 62 percent had held a post then. The orientation, however, was stronger toward the revolutionary tradition; besides the experience in the Revolution, 18 percent began their legislative careers in May 1815, with a total of 36 percent elected in May 1815 and 39 percent holding a post outside the legislature then. All of these figures are highs for any group of the Restoration. The pattern of involvement appeared to be Revolution, One Hundred Days, 1819. The relationship with the Restoration itself was very weak, only 13 percent were first elected in August 1815 and just 30 percent held a post in the Second Restoration.

The social categories corroborated the orientation of the experience pattern. The Old Regime nobility comprised only 10 percent, down from 34 percent in 1816, and it was equally divided between Titled and Nontitled. The Bourgeois increased, but it was the Imperial noble who showed the greatest increase. This group made up 32 percent of those elected, nearly as large a group as in the Corps Législatif of the Empire. The switch from the Old Regime representation to Imperial representation, however, was not a return to the type of man who served in the Napoleonic period, since the Bourgeois was only 29 percent. In 1819 the Imperial noble was simply being substituted for the Old Regime noble.

With respect to the occupations of the deputies, Proprietor continued to be the largest category with 27 percent; yet the orientation toward the period of the Revolution was also in evidence, with Law deputies increased to 25 percent, even though the Government category decreased to 13 percent. This last decline was undoubtedly due to the large number of opposition deputies elected.

In summary, the men of 1819 were not only on the Left, they were men of the Revolution. The Restoration was firmly established by 1819 and the opponents of the regime began to work within it. One factor that must be kept in mind is that this was only a one-fifth election, and thus the total number of men involved was only 56. This meant that the decision by relatively few individuals to seek election could have an effect on the percentage results in this study if they won. Despite this, the large increase in revolutionary experience cannot be ignored. An explanation must be sought beyond the decision of a few prominent men to re-enter politics.

One factor that the deputies themselves credited with aiding the success of the Left was the new electoral law.[5] The single college for each department was believed to favor the Left, and the Left had won. If the voting figures are examined, this conclusion is harder to sustain, since there was an increase in the voter turnout and not a decline as was anticipated. Although it is difficult to tell which segment of the electorate continued to abstain, it was the Right that had the greatest percentage of its deputies elected where over three-quarters of the registered voters participated, and the Left that had the greatest percentage where the turnout was under one-half. This coincided with what the deputies believed; however, these differences between the parties were not very large.

Of those who actually voted, it was the Right that had more of its deputies, 58 percent, receive a bare majority of 56 percent or less of the vote, whereas the Left had only 29 percent of its deputies in this category. This leads me to think that the voter turnout was not the critical factor for the Left's victory. The new law may have had some effect, but this is difficult to see from the voting statistics since these displayed a larger shift to the Left than the new law would have produced.

The movement to the Left was a general one throughout France, but as in the previous elections of the Restoration it followed a regional pattern (see map 8).[6] The East and Champagne remained strong areas for the Left, and the southern third of the country weak areas for the Left. There were, however, certain areas that violated the regional pattern established for the Restoration in 1815–1816. While the North, Channel, and Paris Area regions continued to support the Center as in 1816, the West, Lower West, and Mountain regions swung heavily behind the Left. The latter three regions had an average of 77

[5] Weil, *Les élections*, pp. 92–93.
[6] And see percentages in table 8, Appendix C.

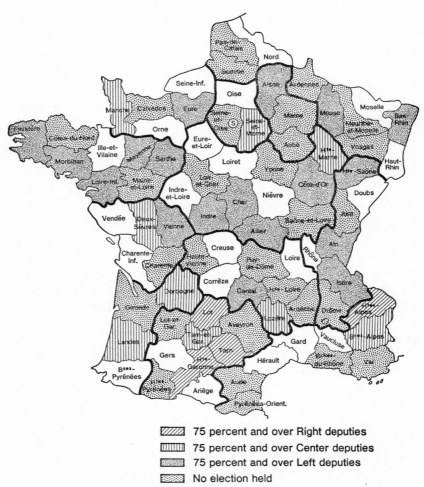

75 percent and over Right deputies
75 percent and over Center deputies
75 percent and over Left deputies
No election held

Map 8.   Elections of 1817–1819, by department.

percent Left deputies compared to the national average of 50 percent, and, more importantly, compared to their own average of 14 percent in 1816. The most extreme change occurred in the Lower West, where there were 14 percent Left deputies in 1816 and 82 percent Left deputies in 1817–1819. Also the South Coast and Center regions moved from strong support of the Right to strong support of the Center. Despite these variations the general Restoration pattern was in evidence, but the Center had lost its position to the Left.

Even though the regional pattern continued in these elections, there were no significant correlations with the SED variables. This means that the various departments of the country voted in a random manner. The lack of significant correlation demonstrates that the unique victory of the Left, with its heavy orientation toward the Revolution, did not have basic economic or demographic causes, at least not any that I was able to measure. The results were the consequence of other changes in society and, as I indicated above, I believe these to be political factors.

The end result of this analysis of the hiatus of 1817–1819 is that historians have not yet found the key to the shift in voter preference. I have said there was a return of men of the Revolution, but I have not said what caused it. The elections of 1819 are famous because of the Abbé Grégoire's success in Isère, and historians have pointed to the frustrations of the Ultras in explaining the victory of the Left since the Ultras did help elect Grégoire. However, the voting statistics show that only 8 percent of the Left deputies won victories of 75 percent or more of the votes cast, and one would expect this figure to be much greater if the combination of Left and Ultra was very prevalent. What no one has yet explained is why the West, Lower West, and Mountains voted so overwhelmingly for the Left and why the country turned to men with a heavy share of revolutionary experience. I personally think the country had overcome the reaction of August 1815 and the devotion to the New France was reasserting itself. Events, including the elections of 1819, made this reassertion only a temporary hiatus in the dominance of the Right during the Restoration.

VII

THE TRIUMPH OF THE RIGHT

Although the victories of the Left in 1817–1819 came in only one-fifth elections, so that the majority of the Chamber remained in support of the government of Decaze, they nevertheless caused concern in the country. The Abbé Grégoire was denied his seat in 1819, because he had sat in the Convention and because he had made his desire for the death of Louis XVI known, although he was absent on the actual vote. Despite the help of the Right in electing Grégoire, its members were furious that such a man could win an election. The fact that Manuel, an ardent Bonapartist, was also elected in two departments in 1818 was also disturbing to the Right. The Left in general used its popularity to try to expand political freedoms. It would not cooperate with Decaze's attempts to pacify it, and the level of political agitation rose.

This movement was not unique to France; Prussia and Austria were undergoing similar problems. By 1819 a reaction appeared to be starting throughout Europe. The Carlsbad decrees were proclaimed by Austria and adhered to by Prussia, and in France Decaze began to move toward the Right. In 1820 he started preparing a new electoral law, which would deny to the Left the supposed benefits of the law of 1817. At this point, February 1820, the Duke de Berry, the second in line to the throne, was assassinated. This act was blamed on the agitation of the Left and the reaction was immediate and severe.[1]

In the Chamber the Center moved into a coalition with the

[1] G. Bertier de Sauvigny, *The Bourbon Restoration* (Philadelphia, 1966), pp. 164–167.

Right. The government brought forward its proposal for the new electoral law and the Right quickly turned this opportunity to its advantage. The end result was the electoral law of 1820, or, as it is usually entitled, the Law of the Double Vote. In order to reduce the advantage of the urban voter, all of the current deputies were given individual districts within their departments. The elections were then held in the main city of the district and not as formerly in the departmental capital. The Right, however, was not satisfied with this simple change. The restrictiveness of the electoral system was therefore increased by adding 172 new seats, for which only the top quarter of the electorate, as determined by the amount of taxes paid, could vote. The new seats were divided by department as previously. The elections for these new seats were to be held one week after the district elections, thus giving the defeated candidates a second chance at election and also allowing time for the double voters to travel to the departmental capital.

None of the qualifications for office or for voting were changed, so the electorate remained at about 100,000 and the eligibles at about 20,000. About 23,000 men had two votes, and the taxes these men paid varied according to the wealth of their department. The minimum probably averaged about 800 francs. For the most part, therefore, the double voters were also the men eligible for office.

The changes in the electoral law were thought to benefit the Right in two ways: by allowing the rural voter to participate more easily, and by giving the wealthier voter more power. After discussing the type of man elected during the conservative triumphs of 1820–1824, I will return to examine the validity of these beliefs.

Whether caused by the new law or not, the voter turnout was overwhelming in 1820. The excitement caused by the assassination of the Duke de Berry and the subsequent birth of his son, the Enfant du Miracle, may have spurred the voters' interest. Whatever the cause, most electors voted in 1820. Over 90 percent of the deputies were elected in areas where the turnout exceeded three-fourths of the registered voters, and over 25 percent of the elections had a turnout of over nine-tenths. This was the first election of the Restoration with such full participation, and the Right was the beneficiary. The Right not only won 83 percent of the seats, it won them by large margins. Only 19 percent of the Right deputies received less than 56 percent of the vote cast, whereas 41 percent of the Left deputies were elected with this narrow margin. In other terms, this meant that 63 percent of the Right deputies had won over 50 percent of the registered voters' support, and thus would have won no matter what the turnout, to only 34 percent for the Left deputies.

Elections were held in 1820 for all of the 172 new seats and also for the normal one-fifth renewal of the old seats. This increased opportunity for office allowed many new men to enter the Chamber; 50 percent of those elected were being elected for the first time in 1820. As one would expect with a group of new legislators, there were fewer old men; only 18 percent were 60 or older—the pre-Revolution generation was dying out. This chronological change, however, did not mean the advocates of the New France were taking their place.

The type of man elected in 1820 closely resembled the type elected in the previous massive victory of the Right in 1815. In fact, 32 percent of the men elected in 1820 had begun their legislative careers in August 1815, and this included a good number who had not served in 1816 to 1819. For example, both the Marquis de Tramecourt and de Lauro followed this pattern. The traditional elites dominated: the Old Regime Titled nobles comprised 35 percent of the deputies and Proprietors comprised 42 percent. The representatives of the New France were pushed aside: the Bourgeois made up only 23 percent and Law only 11 percent.

The experience of the deputies followed the same pattern as the social characteristics. Only 15 percent had held a post during the Revolution and only 6 percent had held one during the One Hundred Days; the emigration was experienced by 22 percent and 19 percent had opposed Napoleon's return. Many men, 44 percent, had still served the Empire, but the bulk of the experience was now to be centered under the Restoration; 46 percent had held a post in the Second Restoration, and during the 1820s 66 percent were going to hold a post.

The rewards of office became more prominent during the 1820s. The Right dominated the government, and these deputies were rewarded for their service. Many deputies on the Right received a post after their election since only 50 percent held a post prior to 1820 compared with 79 percent afterward.

The general profile of the men elected in 1820 corresponds closely to that of those elected in August 1815; this is due primarily to the political affiliation of the deputies. On the Right the only significant variation from the earlier Right groups is in the return to a normal size group of those 60 or older. The voter wanted a turn to the Right in 1815 and in 1820 and both times he chose the same type of man with the same type of experience to accomplish the task.

When the Left underwent a severe reversal of fortunes in 1820, this defeat struck particularly hard on those with a Napoleonic background since the connection between the Left and those who had served Napoleon was reduced. The Imperial noble comprised 29 percent of the Left in 1817–1819, but just 15 percent in 1820, and 60 percent had held a post under the Empire in 1817–1819, but only 44 percent in 1820. This discrimination against Napoleonic men is even clearer when the total number elected in 1820 is examined, because the Right never had as many deputies with Napoleonic experience; so when the success of the Right is included, the total amount of Napoleonic men who were elected in 1820 was small. Only 9 percent had Imperial titles and just 4 percent had sat in the Corps Législatif. It was only experience in Local Administration which inflated those who held a post during Napoleonic times to 44 percent.

The Left had additional changes in 1820. The few who did succeed in being elected were older than previous Left groups; only 31 percent were under 50 compared to 41 percent in the years of victory, and despite this aging they had held fewer posts during the Revolution. Further, the Law deputy on the Left fared particularly poorly in 1820, his share declined to only 13 percent, while the Proprietor became the largest occupational group on the Left, just as it was on the Right. Thus, even when the Left managed to win an election, the voter turned less often to the revolutionary-oriented deputy than it had in 1817–1819.

The change in the political climate caused by the assassination and other political events has already been touched upon, and I think it provides the bulk of the explanation for the results of 1820. There was the new electoral law, however, and its effects can be analyzed. Because there were two sets of deputies in the period 1820–1830, one for the departments and one for the districts, it is easy to analyze the effects of this legal change. While the new law was in force, there were three one-fifth elections—1820, when all the new departmental deputies were elected for the first time, 1821, and 1822—and there were three general elections—1824, 1827, and 1830. During this period there were no further changes in the electoral laws except one in 1824. The one-fifth renewal elections were then ended and the deputies were given concurrent seven-year terms of office. Since the departmental and district elections were conducted under similar political and economic conditions, the influence of the electoral law was the only cause of any differences between the two groups of deputies.

The most conspicuous aspect of the departmental deputies was their support of the Right. The reaction that ensued upon the assassination of the Duke de Berry had enabled the Right to pass the new law with the express purpose of increasing its chances of election.[2] In 1820, when the 172 departmental seats were filled for the first time, the Right won 92 percent of them; however, they won only 57 percent of the district seats being contested that year. In 1821–1822 the political climate had moved further to the Right, with 91 percent of the departmental seats and 69 percent of the district seats won. The favoritism of the double voter for the Right was still apparent (see fig 7).

During the three full elections conducted under the Law of the Double Vote the Right was not favored as much as the Left was discriminated against. In 1824, when the Right won overwhelmingly in both the departmental and district elections, the Left won only 3 percent of the departmental seats as compared to 8 percent of the districts. The change in political conditions in 1827 affected both electorates in an equal manner. The Right gained half of both the departmental and district seats; the Left won only 41 percent of the departmental seats to 47 percent of the district seats. By 1830 the behavior of the two electorates was diverging again; the Right won 48 percent in the departments, but just 24 percent in the districts; the Left won only 45 percent in the departments but 64 percent in the districts.

---

[2] Georges-Denis Weil, *Les élections législatives depuis 1789* (Paris, 1895), pp. 92–93.

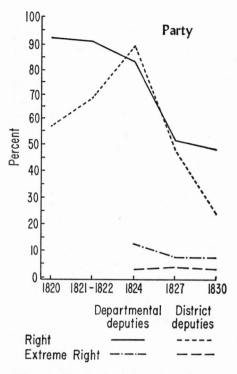

Fig. 7.   Law of the Double Vote.

The new law certainly helped the Right, but it brought radically different results in only 1820 and 1830. No law kept the electorate from changing its mind, since even among "its" voters the Right had fallen into the minority by 1830. The double vote by itself extended the success of the Right through the 1827 election. Nevertheless the July Ordinances, which would have made the double voter the only voter, would not have salvaged the majority for Charles X. The great shift in the voter's attitude occurred in 1827 and the trend toward the Left continued in 1830 everywhere, even if it was much faster among the district voters than the departmental voters.

The various characteristics of the departmental deputies tended to reflect their "party" on the one hand and the voters on the other hand. These deputies were wealthier and more of them were nobles and Proprietors. In 1820 the departmental deputies were 43 percent Titled nobles compared to only 10 percent of such men in the districts; the closest the two groups ever came in this category was a difference of 16 percent in both 1827 and 1830 (see fig. 8). The occupations reflected the social class and thus the Proprietors were favored as departmental deputies. Forty-five percent in 1830 was the lowest figure of Proprietors for the departmental deputies; 38 percent in 1824 was the highest for the district deputies. On the other hand, Business was more favored as an occupation by the district deputies, as compared to the departmental deputies, and the other occupations showed no great preference (see fig. 9). The greater wealth of the departmental deputies did not occur in the Over 5,000 tax category, where the two groups were equal, but in the other categories. There were more departmental deputies than district deputies in the 1,500–4,999 group, and there were more district deputies in the less than 1,500 (see fig. 10).

The departmental seats were a more common place to initiate a career, despite the fact that many deputies managed to win election at the departmental level after having suffered a defeat in their bid for re-election in their district. This occurred most frequently in 1827 and 1830 among Right deputies and was clear evidence that the Law of the Double Vote helped extend the life of the Right. As one might expect when all the seats were new, however, the departmental deputies had a high number of first-time deputies elected in 1820, 55 percent compared to 33 percent in the districts. Only in 1821–1822 and 1824 did the district percentage of first-time elected even approach that for the departments (see fig. 11).

For those deputies previously elected, the departmental deputies followed the pattern of the Right with few elected prior to the Restoration and many first elected in August 1815. The date first elected for the departmental deputies showed that the double voter had a real antipathy toward the men first elected during the One Hundred Days. In 1827 and 1830, when the party affiliation of the departmental deputies was about equal, the number among the departmental deputies who were first-time elected in May 1815 was only one-tenth in 1827 and one-fifth in 1830 of those among the district deputies, whereas those first-time elected in August 1815 for both years was nearly equal.[3]

---

[3] See table 15, Appendix C.

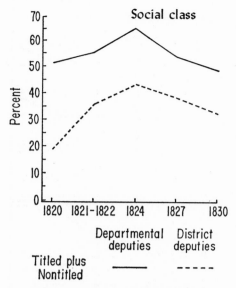

Fig. 8. Law of the Double Vote.

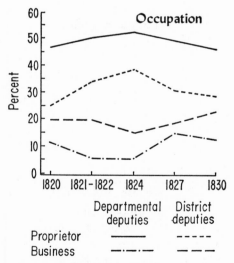

Fig. 9. Law of the Double Vote.

The experience of the deputies of the two groups also indicated this attitude toward the One Hundred Days. Again using 1827, the district deputies had 19 percent who had held a post in the One Hundred Days and the departmental deputies had

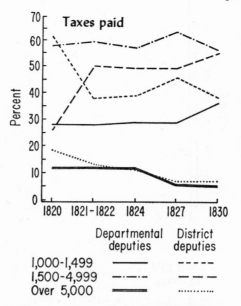

Fig. 10. Law of the Double Vote.

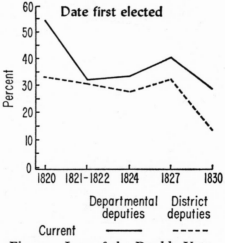

Fig. 11. Law of the Double Vote.

just 5 percent who had held a post in the One Hundred Days
(see fig 12). The departmental deputies of both parties had less
experience in this period than their respective group of district
deputies, thus eliminating party as the cause of the variation be-

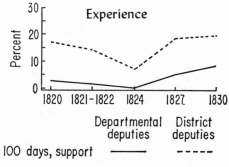

Fig. 12.   Law of the Double Vote.

tween the departmental and district deputies. It is difficult to know how to evaluate this aversion, although the One Hundred Days was a time of disorder and men of wealth usually have a great dislike for disorder. One other possible explanation was the voters' devotion to the monarchy, for combined with their antipathy to men who had betrayed Louis XVIII was a propensity to elect émigrés; only in 1824 and 1827 was the percentage of émigrés among the departmental deputies less than twice that among the district deputies, and then it was still over one-third greater (see fig. 13). Considering the importance of dynastic loyalty voiced by the Left in 1827–1830, the idea that the departmental voters appeared to be dedicated monarchists, whether they voted for men on the Right or on the Left, seems valid.

In summary, a legal influence on the type of man elected did exist. It could not change the direction of the political tide, but it could affect the level of the flow. The wealthy voter favored a more conservative, more aristocratic, and wealthier man as a deputy. This was most noticeable in the high percentage of departmental deputies who were Proprietors. The double voter also had a marked antipathy toward the man with Napoleonic experience, especially one who had been loyal to Napoleon during his return. This quirk explains the anomaly of the low number of deputies with connections to the Napoleonic period in the election of 1820, when only 9 percent were Imperial nobles and only 44 percent had held a post during the Empire, since the double voter elected 77 percent of the deputies in that election. Nevertheless, the evolution of the departmental depu-

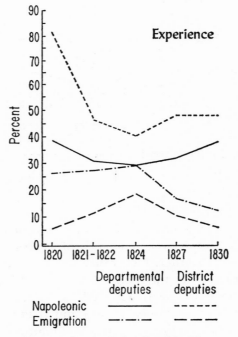

Fig. 13.   Law of the Double Vote.

ties was in the same direction as for the district deputies. By introducing the legal change in 1820 the Right had found a realistic way of affecting political behavior, but it had not found a way of reversing political opinion.

If the electoral law did not cause the switch to the Right in 1820, then some other explanation must be sought. Of the SED variables, none had a significant correlation in 1820. Region continued to be influential, with a pattern similar to those found in previous elections (see map 9).[4] The East, Champagne, and Lower West favored the Left at a level significantly above the national average, and the South, South Coast, Central Mountains, and Mountains favored the Right. The regions North, Channel, and Paris Area switched from a strong support of the Center in 1816 and 1817–1819 to strong support of the Right in 1820. Thus there is little change in these underlying factors and they do not help explain the success of the Right. The political events appear to offer the best explanation and they did seem

[4] And see percentages in table 10, Appendix C.

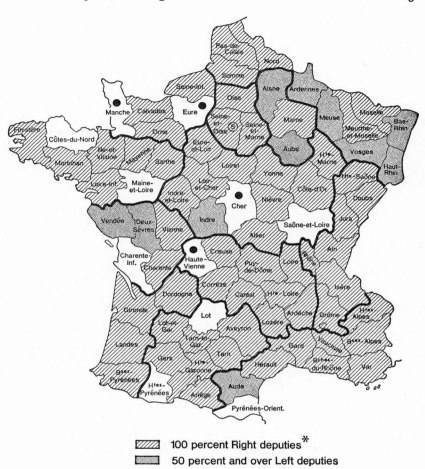

�▨ 100 percent Right deputies[*]
■ 50 percent and over Left deputies

* See note to map 6.

Map 9.   Elections of 1820, by department.

to affect the same areas as the reaction of 1815 had affected, underscoring the other similarities found between the elections of August 1815 and 1820.

By the fall of 1821 and the annual one-fifth elections, which included the new departmental deputies for those departments due for renewal, the political temper was still behind the conservatives. Richelieu had retaken control of the government from Decaze. The health of Louis XVIII was failing, and thus the influence of Monsieur, the Count d'Artois, increased. Richelieu

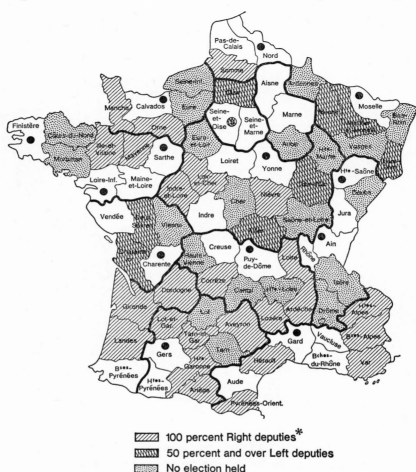

* See note to map 6.

Map 10.   Elections of 1821–1822, by department.

was trying to govern with a Center-Right coalition, but there
was pressure from the Right, including that of Monsieur, to
move even further to the right.[5] The elections proved favorable
to the Right again; it won 79 percent of the seats. A year later
Richelieu was replaced by Joseph de Villèle and the government
was controlled by the Right for the first time since 1815. Also
in 1822, the Right again won with 77 percent of the seats (see
map 10).[6]

[5] S. Charléty, *La Restauration* (Paris, 1921), pp. 158–170.

[6] And see percentages in table 10, Appendix C.

The voter turnout declined in 1821–1822 from its high level of 1820, but it did not return to the low levels existing prior to 1820. Both parties had 58 percent of their deputies elected in areas where over three-quarters of the voters participated. The number of constituencies where over nine-tenths voted decreased on the Right from 27 percent in 1820 to 8 percent in 1821–1822, yet this type of turnout declined only from 26 to 20 percent on the Left. This indicated that a large turnout was critical for the Left, as also a much higher percentage of its deputies won by narrow margins, 32 to 20 percent. On the other hand, the Right, 26 percent of the time, won with over three-quarters of the votes cast compared to only 2 percent of the Left deputies with this great support. Again the Right had won an even more impressive victory than the mere number of seats won would have indicated.

The support of the Right was solid and, like the party affiliation, the type of men elected in 1821–1822 were similar to those elected in 1820, with a few exceptions. The man with the Napoleonic background, who had been discriminated against in 1820, returned in 1821–1822. This change occurred on the Left, where 35 percent were Imperial nobles in 1821–1822. This figure was the highest for any election of the study. I think it was a result of the discrimination by the double voters in 1820, since those men discriminated against in 1820 won election in 1821 and thus created the high percentage of Imperial nobles, 18 percent, in 1821; in 1822 the percentage of Imperial nobles returned to a normal level.

The other noticeable difference in 1821–1822 from 1820 was the rise of status on the Left. I have already noted the increase in Imperial nobles; the Old Regime nobles also increased. Most noticeable, however, was the rise in the percent of Left deputies who paid over 1,500 francs in direct taxes from 46 percent in 1820 to 70 percent in 1821–1822. The increase in both types of nobility probably caused some of this increased wealth, but both wealth and noble status were very likely necessary to overcome the voters' aversion to men of the Left. The experience of the Left deputies supports this idea that a less radical background helped a man get elected. While the percentage of those on the Left who had held a post during the Revolution and the One Hundred Days remained constant between 1820 and 1821–1822,

the percentage of émigrés rose from 3 to 14 percent, those opposing the return of Napoleon rose from zero to 9 percent, and those
who had held a post under Napoleon rose from 44 to 65 percent.
The Left, without abandoning its commitment to the New
France, had won with men of higher status and a more varied
background.

Failing to win very many seats, even with the more conservative type man, the more radical leaders of the Left looked to
overthrow the regime. Lafayette and others planned a coup
d'état which aborted in 1822. With this extraparliamentary failure, in combination with the successful war in Spain—for which
the Left had predicted disaster—and a favorable economic situation, the government called for new elections in 1824 in which
the Left was completely decimated: the Right won 85 percent
of the seats and the Left only 8 percent. The counteropposition,
which was forming on the Extreme Right, accounted for the
other 7 percent.

The victory of the Right brought about the most conservative Chamber of the Restoration in the type of men elected,
even surpassing the men of the Chambre Introuvable; 39
percent were Old Regime Titled nobles and 43 percent were
Proprietors, and Law and Business were only 7 percent and
11 percent respectively. The experience of the Revolution was
down to just 13 percent, but the percent of émigrés was at its
highest point, 24 percent. The holding of a post under Napoleon
was at its lowest point, 35 percent, as was the holding of a post
during the One Hundred Days, 4 percent; 19 percent had been
opposed to Napoleon's return and 48 percent had held a post
during the Second Restoration. The spoils of office also were
open to these men: 71 percent had at least one honor and 81
percent held a post outside of the Chamber in the 1820s. Finally,
this conservatism was not a product of any older generation,
since in 1822 40 percent of the deputies elected were born after
1769 and in 1824 this jumped to 54 percent. The younger generation was not being excluded from power, but only a certain
type of man was appealing to the voter in 1824.

Despite the overall conservative profile of the men elected in
1824, the profile of the Right showed virtually no changes from
the previous Right groups except in the rewards of office, whereas the men on the Left who survived the debacle of 1824 had

peculiar profiles. Eighty-two percent of the Right held a post during the 1820s and 64 percent held the Legion of Honor; these two categories had been 75 and 50 percent respectively in 1821–1822. The Left, on the other hand, had its greatest number of Old Regime Titled nobles, 21 percent, in 1824, a high number, 27 percent, of Military men, and only 13 percent Proprietors, since the usual association of Titled nobles with the Proprietor category was not true in 1824. The climate created by the military escapades in Spain undoubtedly helped Military men of all political persuasions.

Another oddity of the Left in 1824 was that the men who began their legislative careers before the Restoration increased to 45 percent while those with experience of these same periods declined. Napoleonic experience was down to 47 percent at the same time experience of the later periods rose; the men who held a post in the 1820s increased to 44 percent. Certainly 1824 was a bad time for someone on the Left to try to begin a career, since only 18 percent of the Left were being elected for the first time. This helps explain why the Left had few young men, only 27 percent were under 50 years old. The voters' favoritism for the Right appeared to be overcome by either a long legislative career or a willingness to serve the regime.

All of this came about when there was a large turnout; the Right had 72 percent of its deputies and the Left had 88 percent of its deputies elected where over three-fourths of the registered voters participated. The Left again fared best when turnout was the largest, 49 percent of its deputies were elected when the turnout was over 90 percent while the Right, on the other hand, had only 15 percent of its deputies elected in this type of district. The large participation for the Left was often crucial, 44 percent of its deputies received slim majorities or less than 56 percent while the Right had only 17 percent of its deputies with this slight margin. The tremendous voter interest had not hurt the Right, 70 percent of the Right deputies had received over half of the registered vote, but the large turnout did allow the Left to win a few more seats than they otherwise would have won.

This victory of the Right in 1824 has been ascribed to the triumphs in Spain and to the increased use of the power of the government to influence the elections. Charléty believed the government's tactics were instrumental in its victory.[7] On the surface this was true. Besides using the influence of the presidents of the electoral colleges, open voting so there was a clear threat of withholding government patronage for opposition voting, and other pressures, the government had posted the electoral lists as late as 4:00 A.M. on the day of the election, so no challenges could be made.[8] I have already mentioned, however, that the Right won such great majorities that tactics such as these would seem to carry little weight on the final results.

Louis Girard also claims that such influences were important, especially in the small districts.[9] Again, I feel he is mistaken about 1824, since the government usually did better in the small districts. In 1824 the Right won 86 percent of the small districts, those with less than 300 voters, and in 1827 it won 54 percent (see fig. 14). Thus, in 1824 when the Right won 85 percent of the total seats it won only 1 percent more in these districts, and in 1827 when the Right won only 49 percent of the total seats it won 5 percent more in these small districts. Therefore, the pressure from the government, if it was the motivating force behind the voters in the small districts, was apparently stronger in 1827. Since we know the pressure was greater in 1824, the effect of government pressure was not the cause of the Right's victory in 1824.

Another indication of governmental influence was the use of the presidents of the electoral colleges as official candidates of the government. The king appointed these men and provided them with several thousand francs for the expenses of conducting the elections.[10] In 1824 the presidents who were candidates enjoyed their greatest success: 235 deputies had been president of their electoral college. Only 3 of these men were on the Left. Despite the fact that the remainder made up 59 percent of the Right and 54 percent of the chamber, this influence was still not the cause of their success. In 1827 and 1830 the number of presidents who were elected declined to 98, then to 54, and their per-

---

[7] Charléty, *La Restauration*, pp 195–196.

[8] André Mater, "Le groupement régional des partis politiques à la fin de la Restauration," *La Révolution française* 42 (1902): 415.

[9] Louis Girard, *Le libéralisme en France de 1814 à 1848* (Paris, 1967), pp. 46–49.

[10] Weil, *Les élections*, p. 125.

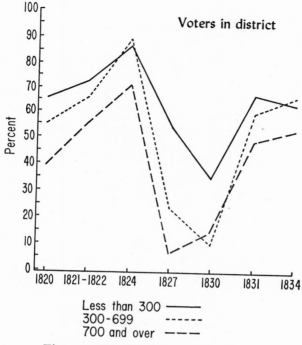

Fig. 14.   The Right, by district size.

centage of the chamber declined to 23, then 12 percent (see fig. 15). The significance of this was that the percentage of the presidents was declining faster than the percentage of the Right. If this type of pressure were successful, the percent of presidents would decrease more slowly than the percent of the Right.

Charléty found an active government influence in 1824 and a great government victory, and he then assumed one caused the other. Girard made the same error in regard to the small districts. They both ignored the fact that the same type of pressure in other elections did not have the same results. The governmental influence in 1824 appears to have been a scapegoat for the Left to explain its failures with the voters, and most historians have agreed with this analysis.

What was clear by the mid–1820s was the voters' favoritism for the traditional elite as deputies. Among them were men like the Marquis de Tramecourt and de Lauro who were first elected in August 1815, were returned to the Chamber as departmental deputies in 1820, and were re-elected in 1824. Another example

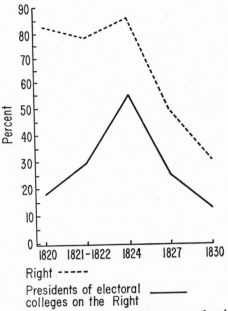

Right `- - - -`
Presidents of electoral ———
colleges on the Right

Fig. 15.   Government influence on elections.

is Pierre Béraud des Renard, a Near noble because his father had
been a royal counselor, a Proprietor in Allier, and president of
the district college that elected him in 1824. He supported the
government and in both 1827 and 1830 he was defeated at the
district election before being re-elected by the departmental college. Another new man was Jacques Miron de Lespinay, a Near
noble because his father also had been a royal counselor, who was
president of the civil tribunal when he was elected by the departmental college of Loiret. Only 42 years old, Miron de Lespinay had been in the magistrature since the Second Restoration
and had been awarded the Legion of Honor in 1821. This would
be his only election. There were many men from the magistrature elected, but the deputies with Law as an occupation, which
has been closely identified with the Revolution, showed little
success in this period. Even the Left deputies were less revolutionary oriented in their characteristics. The success of the Right
was not repeated again during the Restoration, and it is this shift
in electoral fortunes which needs explaining.

The regionalism of the first years of the Restoration main-

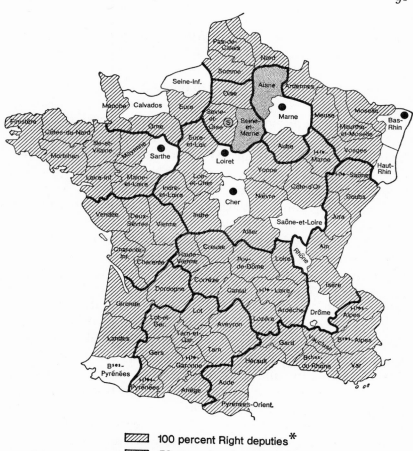

100 percent Right deputies*
50 percent and over Left deputies

* See note to Map 6.

Map 11. Elections of 1824, by department
(the Extreme Right is excluded).

tained itself in the early 1820s, but with some slight variations
(see map 11).[11] The Paris Area led the way in abandoning the
Right. In 1820 it had voted 100 percent for the Right; in 1821–
1822 it voted only 45 percent for the Right, and its 55 percent for
the Left was over twice the national average of 23 percent. In
1824 the Paris Area, as representative of the nation, voted a high
Right majority, but this region increased its discrepancy vis-
à-vis the nation, as the Paris Area's 19 percent of Left deputies

[11] And see percentages in table 10, Appendix C.

was triple the national average. At 19 percent the trend that this region was developing did not really show itself, but as most other regions moved away from the Left between 1820 and 1824, the trend definitely existed. Another region that deviated was the Lower West, which was loyal to the Left at twice the national average in 1821–1822; but this loyalty ended in 1824, when no Left deputies were successful. The East also moved away from the Left. In 1820 it favored the Left at four times the average; in 1821–1822 its favoritism was reduced to below twice the average, and in 1824 to just barely above the average. The Champagne region which favored the Left in 1820 at over twice the national average, however, maintained its traditional orientation toward the Left in these years.

The Right retained its established areas of strength in 1821–1822 and in 1824 these reached monumental proportions. The South voted 100 percent for the Right and the Aquitaine, North, and Lower West regions divided their deputies between the Right and the Extreme Right with no Left deputies elected.

Below this continued regionalism a new pattern of correlations developed with the SED variables. In 1817–1819 and 1820 no SED variable had a significant correlation; in 1821–1822 *Percent literate, Students,* and *Patentes* had significant correlations. These correlations were all negative with the Right, so that the socially backward and now the less commercial areas were the strongest supporters of the Right and conversely the more educated and commercially active areas supported the Left.

The great victory of the Right in 1824 furthered the shift in the SED factors. The *Student* factor no longer had a significant correlation, but *Percent literate* and *Patentes* plus *Industrial production, Industrial workers, Population of communes, Percent population change,* and the four variables that measured wealth all had significant negative correlations with the Right and positive ones with the Left. What this means is that the few areas that voted for the Left were the wealthier and more advanced areas of France. This explains the high amount, 32 percent, of Business deputies on the Left in 1824.

Underlying the victory of the Right, therefore, was potential disaster, since the growing and wealthy areas were not being won over. In the glory of prosperity and military victory this meant little, for the Right had won an astounding triumph, but the men of the Old France, who inhabited the Right's benches in the Chamber, would rule the New France for only a few more years. The election of 1824 was the high point of conservatism, but the traditional elites were already being undermined in their hour of glory.

VIII

VICTORY FOR PROGRESS
AND MODERATION

Shortly after the victory of the Right in 1824 Louis XVIII died
and his brother and leader of the Ultras, the Count d'Artois,
ascended the throne as Charles X. His coronation aroused fears
among some of a return to the Old Regime. As seen earlier, the
areas that had voted against the Right were the more progressive
and wealthy areas. These areas' disenchantment with the policies
of the government went unnoticed in 1824, but in the next six
years the disenchantment would spread to a majority of the
electorate and culminate in the Revolution of 1830.

In 1824 the Right sought to take advantage of its great triumph by ending the one-fifth renewal elections and replacing
them with one general election every seven years. This, of course,
would allow the Right to maintain control until at least 1831.
Events, however, were to force the government to dissolve the
Chamber three times before then, each time with worse results
for the government and its party, the Right. The Chamber was
dissolved in 1827, when the government nearly lost its majority,
in 1830, when the government failed to receive a majority, and
again after the elections of June 1830, when the Chamber refused to be dissolved and instead overthrew the government.
This period forms a cohesive whole. The Left not only triumphed, but it did so on a new basis. The members of the Left
were more moderate in their profiles than earlier Left groups
and the type of department that elected them continued the
trend begun in the election of 1824.

In 1824 no hint existed of the problems waiting ahead for the government of Villèle. He had his "300," and he could begin to solve some long-standing social problems. The question of the lands seized and sold by the government during the Revolution was settled without arousing too much bitterness by guaranteeing their sale and granting the original owners an indemnity.[1] The aristocrat-dominated Chamber made the remainder of society shoulder most of the burden, but the issue of the national lands was settled without reversing their sale or breaking the state financially.[2] Villèle was not, however, to achieve success in his other ventures. Almost immediately after the election, he suffered the rupture with Chateaubriand. This was primarily a personal matter, yet it diminished the government's popularity and caused an elegant voice to join the fast-coalescing counter-opposition, which found itself moving toward a coalition with the Left.

The government's main problem, though, arose over religion. Until this issue emerged in 1825, the Left and the Right were clearly separated.[3] Every issue on which they disagreed divided them into two distinct groups. The Church issue, however, raised two problems for the government. On the one hand, it raised fears for diminished religious freedom, especially in areas like Alsace where there were substantial numbers of non-Catholics,[4] and on the other hand, it raised the old Gallican-Ultramontane split, which in turn cut across the Revolution–anti-Revolution split that had separated the deputies until this time. The Left thereafter exploited the Church issue to wean Right deputies favoring Gallicanism away from the government, and it was successful.[5]

Besides the personal and religious problems the government was weakened when it raised fears for equality with its proposals in 1826 on the Law of Heredity, but Villèle's coup de grace was

[1] The success was limited by one's own insecurity. That is, if one feared a return to the Old Regime even this new settlement might be overturned. This insecurity, of course, was heightened for many in 1829–1830.

[2] G. Bertier de Sauvigny, *The Bourbon Restoration* (Philadelphia, 1966), pp. 369–374.

[3] S. Charléty, *La Restauration* (Paris, 1921), p. 253.

[4] Leuilliot, *L'Alsace au début du XIXe siècle* (Paris, 1959), 1:469, 3: passim.

[5] Charléty, *La Restauration*, p. 253.

caused by his own speciality, finances. In 1826–1827 the economy went into a decline and Villèle's fiscal solution for the indemnity of raising the money by lowering the interests on government bonds ran into difficulty.[6] Economic problems will usually reflect badly on the government. The added burden of the reconversion of the government bonds for the indemnity only exacerbated the situation and provided, along with the rupture with Chateaubriand, the revised spectre of a return to the Old Regime, and the religious issue, ample cause for the success of the opposition in the election of 1827, called by the king before the erosion of the government's popularity went any further. The election proved as unfortunate for Villèle, who was dismissed as the chief minister immediately after the election, as for the Right, which won just 49 percent of the seats.

Historians of the Restoration have explained in part the great decline of the Right from 85 percent in 1824 to 49 percent in 1827 by the conflict within the Right, although they have mistakenly treated the political groupings as modern cohesive parties. Since the religious issue and other problems of the government account for how Villèle's "300" disintegrated, historians have assumed that they also explain why the voters switched parties.

I believe studying the type of man elected can take us beyond this old reasoning. As I demonstrated, in 1817–1819 the Left had won with a revolutionary-oriented deputy and the level of revolutionary activity in society rose. This activity rose beyond what the electorate desired, however, and more than that it was blamed for causing the assassination of the Duke de Berry. The Left, however, did not acquiesce in the reaction, but instead took its revolution to the streets.[7] It was defeated, and with the success of the government in the Spanish War the electorate went solidly in favor of the Right. Between 1824 and 1827, though, the Left changed its image and its representatives. The electorate wanted neither reaction nor revolution and Stanley Mellon in his *Political Uses of History* has made clear how the Left historians, like Guizot, wrote their histories in order to picture the Left of the Restoration as the conserver of the Revolution as

---

[6] Bertier de Sauvigny, *The Bourbon Restoration*, p. 391.

[7] Ibid., pp. 181–184.

embodied in the Charter of 1814 and to picture Charles X as the revolutionary for wanting to change the Charter.[8] This picturing of themselves as conservatives by the spokesmen of the Left was more than rhetoric, for the men of the Left who were successful in 1827 had a different and a more moderate profile than the Left had had earlier.

The Left of 1827 had suddenly grown old. Although the number born before 1770 had been 67 percent in 1817–1819, it was still 36 percent in 1827. Compare these figures with those for the Right, where in 1817–1819 71 percent were born before 1770 but in 1827 only 15 percent were born then. The relatively small decrease on the Left in men born before 1770 was also accompanied by a much larger, 60 percent, reduction in experience in the Revolution. That is, the men in 1827 were old enough to have served in the Revolution, but they had not done so. There was more than just a reduction in the amount of experience, however; emigration also played a part. The ratio between experience in the Revolution and emigration was 8 to 1 for the Left of 1817–1819 and only 3 to 1 for the Left of 1827. Further, the Left of 1817–1819 had a 13 to 1 ratio of support for the return of Napoleon, but the Left of 1827 had only a 2.5 to 1 ratio. The moderation of the Left of 1827 was in evidence in its social composition too. Twenty-two percent were Old Regime nobles in 1827 as compared to 10 percent in 1817–1819, and the occupations of Law and Professions were down to 12 percent in 1827 compared to 30 percent in 1817–1819. The Left, then, had turned away from the radical of 1817–1819 toward a more moderate type of man, and it had won. The electorate appeared ready to give power to moderates on the Left.

As I will discuss later, many men on the Left began their careers in the Chamber of 1827. Firmin Didot (b.1764), a publisher, and Casimir Duffour-Dubesson (b.1775), a *negociant* from Bordeaux, were two such men. Neither man has any recorded political involvement before his election by the opposition in 1827. One who does was Jacques Mercier, a Baron of the Empire and

[8] Stanley Mellon, *The Political Uses of History* (Stanford, 1958). Also see Charles Dupin, *Forces productives et commerciales de la France* (Bruxelles, 1828), for a good example of a contemporary trying to make progress safe—that is, so it would not destroy society as it was known at the time.

a manufacturer. He had served as a mayor during the Empire and as a deputy in the One Hundred Days. These men are fairly typical of the new type of man elected on the Left.

As the Left had become more moderate in victory, the Right also had a slight movement toward moderation in defeat. Maintaining its basic profile, but with more Imperial nobles, the significant change for the Right came in those who had experience of the Revolution: those who had held a post increased and those who had emigrated declined. The increase is especially significant because the Right had more young members in 1827 than it had in 1824; those under 50 had increased and those over 60 had decreased from 1824 to 1827. This movement on the Right and the moderation of the Left both support Felix Ponteil's claim that the settlement of the national lands question helped the country put the past behind them.[9] That is, the experience of the revolutionary era was becoming less divisive for the parties.

The changes in the parties internally and the change in their relative strengths led to a new profile for the total Chamber in 1827. There was a decline in the Titled nobles and the Proprietors, which coincided with the decrease in the Right. The connections to the Restoration itself were also diminished. Fewer men had been first-elected in August 1815 and, in fact, for the first time this group failed to be the largest group of experienced legislators. The experience of the deputies in the three periods of the Restoration was also less than in 1824, but the experience of the Napoleonic period rose. To better understand the changes that occurred in 1827 it is best to examine the type of men who were not re-elected then and compare them with the men who were elected in 1827.

There is a wide discrepancy in the characteristics of the 259 deputies eliminated in 1827 and the 429 deputies elected in 1827. The party percentages were fairly close to those of the Chamber in which each group served, which meant that most of those eliminated were on the Right, 93 percent, whereas just 49 percent of the new men were on the Right. As expected, the

9 Felix Ponteil, *Les institutions de la France de 1814 à 1870* (Paris, 1966), p. 55. Note that when the fears of reaction were stimulated in 1829–1830 this process was momentarily halted.

men leaving were old, especially on the Right; 43 percent of the eliminated Right and 40 percent of the eliminated Left were over 60. The gerontocracy that contemporaries complained about, however, was not being reduced in this election, since of those elected 28 percent were over 60 years old as compared to 24 percent in 1824. This was especially true of the Left where 32 percent were over 60 years old.[10]

The move away from the traditional elites for the total Chamber of 1827, which one would expect from a Left victory, occurred; so there were more traditional elites among those leaving than among those newly elected, but when each party group of the total new Chamber and of those eliminated is analyzed separately, there was a greater percentage of the traditional elites in each party among the new men than among those being eliminated. Of those being eliminated 10 percent of the Left and 50 percent of the Right were Old nobility, and of the new men 22 percent of the Left and 61 percent of the Right were of the Old nobility.[11]

As in 1816, the excess of military men that the victories of the Right had fostered was eliminated and the Business deputy made large gains. The Military deputies composed 18 percent of those eliminated which reduced their share of the Chamber in 1827 to 12 percent. The increase in the Business deputies occurred because of the great increase in the Left where Business deputies were very popular. Just 10 percent of those eliminated and 28 percent of those elected were in Business.

The experience of the two groups, which has sharp changes in certain areas and little changes in others, shows the moderation of the new men as well as the shift from a Right-dominated Chamber to one where the Left held a large place. Among those elected the experience in the Revolution was not as great as expected, as it was only equal to that of those being eliminated. The experience of the Napoleonic period was also fairly close for the two groups and a relatively large number of those elected, 13 per-

---

[10] J.-J. Fazy, *De la gérontocratie ou abus de la sagesse des vieillards dans le gouvernement de la France* (Paris, 1828).

[11] This apparent impossibility occurs because among the new men the rise in Old Nobles is not large enough to offset the fact that so many of the new men are on the Left where the percent of Old nobility was small.

cent, had opposed Napoleon's return. Within this moderation, however, the shift to a Left-oriented pattern of experience is also present—27 percent of those eliminated had been émigrés compared to 14 percent of those elected. The shift to a Left-oriented pattern of experience is particularly evident with regards to 1815, when the experience of the One Hundred Days was just 4 percent of those eliminated who had held a post compared to 14 percent of those elected. Only 2 percent of those eliminated had begun their legislative careers during the One Hundred Days whereas 8 percent of those elected had done so. For the Second Restoration, 26 percent of those eliminated had begun their legislative careers then, and the comparable figure for those elected was only 13 percent. Thus the generation of August 1815 was seriously undermined in 1827.

It should be expected that those leaving office would have enjoyed the rewards of supporting the government, since most of them were on the Right, and this was true. Forty-nine percent had held a post in the Second Restoration and 77 percent in the 1820s. For those elected in 1827, however, only 36 percent had held a post in the Second Restoration and 63 percent in the 1820s. These latter figures were very high for a group composed of a large number of Left deputies. It reflects, I think, a willingness to support the Restoration, if only the government would have them. Many of these men held a post during the Decaze or Martignac ministries when many of the Center-Left deputies supported the government. This possibility of serving in the government was quickly ended by Charles X when he appointed the Polignac ministry in August 1829; as we see later, the willingness to serve this monarchy would not always be present.

The appointment of Prince de Polignac ended the hopes many had nurtured that the government would allow liberty. During the period of the Martignac ministry the *Courrier*, an Alsatian paper that supported the Left, said on 1 January 1829:

> We hope, therefore, that 1829 will see us accomplish what was begun in 1828. . . . The year 1828 had witnessed an event of great importance: the fall of the Villèle ministry. . . . Henceforth the citizens will know that they have only to listen to themselves in order to reverse an administration that was fatal to the country and that the throne is not deaf

to the wishes of the nation, when it expresses them with accord and immunity.[12]

The same paper welcomed Polignac with the words, "We fall again under the yoke of jesuitism and despotism."[13] There was deep devotion to both liberty and the monarchy in these years, but the action of the king forced many to choose between them. The men of the Extreme Left had no problem, but this was not a large group either within or without the Chamber as earlier events had shown. It was the large middle of the political spectrum who had to make the choice; and in 1828–1829 it was clear that the middle had moved forward and it would not be denied its rights. It was the Charter that represented these rights, and this attitude was well expressed by one of the leaders of the Left, Benjamin Constant, when he proclaimed to a crowd in Strasbourg, "La Charte, rien que la Charte, et toute la Charte."[14] The opposition prepared to resist the new government by refusing to pass the budget, since they commanded a majority in the Chamber by late 1829, and if necessary by not paying taxes. The confrontation came at the opening of the parliamentary session in March 1830. The opposition voted to reject the king's address to the opening of the session, which caused Charles X to dissolve the Chamber and call for new elections.

In these elections the Left made a second increase in popularity; if the men elected in 1830 are examined they look very much like the men elected in 1827, except that only 30 percent of the new men were on the Right. They were young, again essentially on the Right, with about the same proportion of the Left and Right from Old Regime noble families as among those elected in 1827. Holding to the existence of more nonrevolutionary oriented deputies, in 1830 Law again was the occupation of few deputies, the two experiences of the One Hundred Days were 15 percent in support and 11 percent in opposition to Napoleon, and as in 1827 there was high experience for both par-

---

[12] Quoted in Leuilliot, *L'Alsace au début*, 1:506.

[13] Ibid., 1:511.

[14] Jean Vidalenc, *Le département de l'Eure sous la monarchie constitutionnelle 1814–1848* (Paris, 1952), p. 276.

[15] Quoted in Leuilliot, 1:473.

ties during the 1820s. Thus, despite the greater outward signs of discontent with the government in 1828–1830, the significant change had occurred prior to the elections of 1827, as demonstrated by the similarities between the deputies elected in 1827 and 1830.

The results of the elections of 1827 and 1830 were no fluke; voter participation reached its high point in these two elections. The Left had 95 percent of its deputies elected where over three-quarters of the registered voters participated in 1827 and the Right had 70 percent in this category. In 1830 these figures increased to 96 and 92 percent respectively. The turnout was particularly great in 1830—both parties had over 35 percent of their deputies elected where the turnout was over nine-tenths (see fig. 16). The campaign of 1830 sparked the interest of the electorate as no other one had before.

The Left benefited from the existence of the society *Aide-toi le Ciel t'aidera* in these elections. This society was formed in 1827 in order to prevent the type of electoral abuses the government perpetrated in 1824.[16] The society was to inspect the voter lists in order to safeguard the opposition from being defeated by illegal voters. After the Left won in 1827, the government of Martignac attempted to placate the Left by making this job of inspection easier. The lists of juries, which also served as the electoral lists, were to be posted each August 15 and to be open to challenge until October 15. Before this time the lists were compiled for each election, and they could be posted any time before the actual voting took place. The society was credited with obtaining removals or additions involving 15,000 names by 1830.[17]

This activity, however, was not the primary basis for the success of the Left. In the overwhelming turnouts of these years, it was the Right that won more seats with a bare majority. In 1827 it had 39 percent of its deputies receive less than 56 percent of the vote; the Left had just 26 percent in this category. In terms of the registered voters, the Right had 34 percent in 1827 and 62 percent in 1830 who received a majority, and the Left had

[16] Georges-Denis Weil, *Les élections législatives depuis 1789* (Paris, 1895), p. 136, and Charles Pouthas, *Guizot pendant la Restauration* (Paris, 1923), pp. 369–380.

[17] Bertier de Sauvigny, *The Bourbon Restoration*, p. 390.

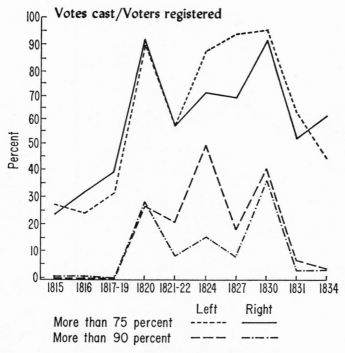

Fig. 16. Voter participation, by party.

55 and 73 percent in the two elections who received a majority of the registered voters. Thus, by 1830 the various districts seemed strongly committed to one party or the other and the changing of a small percentage of the vote would not have helped either side. The electorate had gone through a basic transformation after 1824. In 1824 not only was the Right the victor, but it won with large majorities; in 1830 the Left was the victor, and it had the large majorities.

This transformation had definite regional as well as SED factors underlying it. The regional pattern for 1827 and 1830 was basically the same, but there were substantial differences from 1824 (see maps 12 and 13).[18] Several regions followed the national trend of voting for the Right in 1824 and then the Left in 1827. The areas that deviated from the national average are of interest here. The Paris Area led the stampede to the Left. It had voted Left since 1821 compared to the national average, and it con-

[18] And see percentages in table 12, Appendix C.

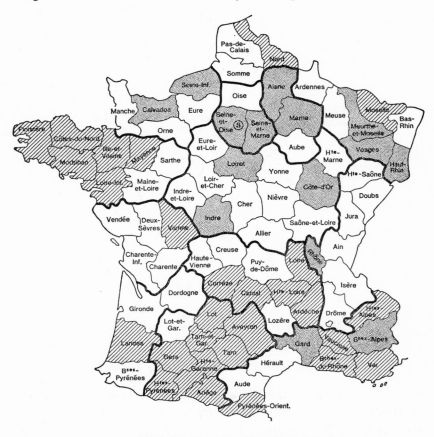

    75 percent and over Right deputies
    75 percent and over Left deputies
Map 12.   Elections of 1827, by department.

tinued to do so in 1827 and also in 1830 when favoritism for the
Left reached 100 percent. Champagne continued its devotion to
the Left, and two new regions, Channel and Center, supported
the Left well above the national average in 1827 and 1830. Also
the old bastion of the Left, the East, and a new region, the South
Coast, definitely favored the Left in 1830 after having voted
much closer to the national average in 1827. As for the Right, it
continued to be sustained at above the national average in its
traditional regions of the North, West, South, Central Mountains, and Aquitaine. The Lower West again had a heavy vote
for the Extreme Right, but without a corresponding average
share of their seats for the Right.

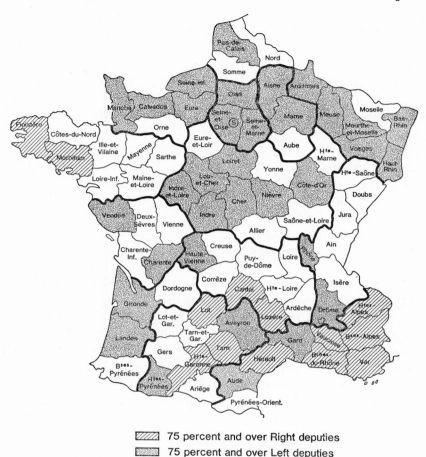

ZZZZ 75 percent and over Right deputies

░░░░ 75 percent and over Left deputies

Map 13. Elections of 1830, by department.

It is important to understanding the results of 1827 and 1830 that the regional distribution be examined closely. In 1817–1819 the Left won 50 percent of the total seats and the Center won 37 percent. In 1827 and 1830 the Left won 44 percent and then 60 percent, but because of the polarization in the political situation there was no Center party. In 1817–1819 the Paris Area, Channel, and Center had voted heavily for the Center; in 1827 they voted for the Left. This well may explain the moderation of the Left in 1827 compared to 1817–1819. The only regions actually to change their position in the two periods of Left victories, and these changes were all away from the Left, were the West, which voted 79 percent for the Left in 1817–

1819 but only 20 percent in 1827 and 33 percent in 1830; the Lower West and Mountains, which went from heavy support of the Left in 1817–1819 to close to the national average in the later period; and the North, which voted for the Center in 1817–1819 and at above the average for the Right in 1827 and 1830. Thus the moderation of the Right in 1827 and 1830 is also partially explained by the regional analysis; besides the switch of the North both Aquitaine and the South had voted above the average for the Center in 1817–1819 and then transferred their support to the Right in 1827 and 1830. What is clear above all is that the country was polarizing around two parties, which were attracting men who were closer to each other in their characteristics.

Even though the Left greatly increased its popularity in the elections of 1827 and 1830 over the election of 1824, the type of areas that supported the Left remained the same. The correlations reach their highest point for most of the variables in 1827. *Patentes* had a correlation of 0.463 with the Left in 1827 and the four measures of wealth, *Industrial production, Population of communes*, and *Percent literate* also had significant correlations then. Besides *Population of communes* these same variables plus *Industrial workers* fell into this category in 1830. The Left, therefore, not only continued to win the wealthier and more advanced areas of France, but the relationship was being strengthened as the Left gained popularity. The cluster analysis discussed earlier also demonstrates the connection between the measures of progress and voting for the Left in the period 1824 to 1830.

This orientation is not only important for what it says about the health of the government of Charles X, but it helps explain the strong position of the Business deputy on the Left. By 1827 the Restoration had split the country and the areas that looked forward dominated. The Left managed to put forth both the rhetoric of moderation and the type of man to sustain such rhetoric, and it took advantage of the government's problems. Historians have long believed that there were basic historical causes for certain regions opposing Charles X; although I have not identified these causes, I have now shown at least what some of the underlying factors were. I cannot claim these social-economic-demographic factors as causes, but they do present another avenue to an understanding of the fall of the Bourbons.

Furthermore, I believe that the more traditional orientation of the Left deputies provided the main clue to the success of the Left in 1827 and 1830. The Left became the protector of what France wanted: the benefits of the Revolution without its chaos. Charléty credited the new generation with producing the change, but even in his own statistics on the electorate he defeated his case.[19] The new generation had to wait for the July Revolution, for the Restoration was still in the hands of the generation of the Revolution of 1789[20] and the Left was the party of the older men whose desire it was to conserve the Revolution that won it popularity. Society was moving forward and Charles X seemed to be moving backward; this was not favored even by the double voters. The conflict in 1827 and 1830 was still over the Revolution, the old versus the new—the new generation would have a post-Revolution outlook and their conflict would not split along the Old Regime definition of class. The voters were not pursuing revolution in the years before 1830, but conservatism. There was a dedication to the idea of the Restoration, but not to Charles X's version of it; the reaction of Charles X led to the July Revolution, which had the acceptance of the vast majority of the electorate. The disappearance of the Old Right after the July Revolution was proof of the position of the electorate: the July Revolution introduced to power the new generation with its new definition of the conflicts within society.

[19] Charléty, *La Restauration*, pp. 197–198.

[20] This did not preclude the presence of men from the post-Revolution generation. One of the chief spokesmen of the idea of a new generation attached to progress, Pierre-Charles Dupin, was elected in 1827 and 1830. See his *Forces productives*.

IX

A NEW BEGINNING

The revolution of July marked an end for a particular type of deputy and the beginning for a new generation of deputies. The noble proprietor who was an émigré was a stereotype of the old deputy. He had been dying of old age before 1830 but with the July Revolution even his son, who had been supplementing him, was not to continue in politics with any success. The new deputy was bourgeois with experience of the Napoleonic period, if he had been old enough to serve the Empire. By comparing those who resigned in 1830 with those elected to replace them, and then those eliminated in 1831 with those first-elected in 1831, the dramatic change that took place can best be described.

The political climate of the country had changed in 1830. The July Revolution made the Revolution of 1789 legitimate. Order was kept in 1830, unlike during 1793 and during the One Hundred Days. Charles X had spent all the goodwill history had provided him, and the Bourbons and the Old Regime were finished; France had moved into the nineteenth century, and this could no longer be denied. The regional examination will show this to be true, but here the focus is on the profiles of the deputies.

The successful and relatively orderly revolution of July had gained the confidence of the people; the electorate would vote a new type of man into office in 1831 and continue with the new type in 1834. The basic conflict in politics shifted from the old one of the Revolution versus the Old Regime to the new one of at what point the Revolution should be halted.[1] The deputies

[1] S. Charléty, *La Monarchie de Juillet* (Paris, 1920), pp. 4–11.

elected in October 1830 were similar to the Left deputies of 1827 and 1830, but by the election of June 1831 the new deputy was a totally different type of man. The old type of deputy of the Restoration would never return, even though the traditional elite maintained a place in the Chamber and he would win back a further share of the Chamber once the Legitimists stopped boycotting the elections and the traditional elite decided to move forward with the New France.[2]

After the July Revolution the deputies had to swear allegiance to the new Charter. Some deputies refused and resigned, some refused and were denied their seats by the Chamber, and some were denied their seats because the Chamber felt their elections had been won by fraud. There were 99 such cases in total, all men on the Right. These were not particularly old men—39 percent were under 50 years old and only 16 percent were over 60. They were, however, from the traditional elite—61 percent were Old Regime nobles and 47 percent were Proprietors. Only 3 percent were in Law and 7 percent in Business. Surprisingly many had begun their careers late—34 percent in 1827 and 21 percent in 1830. Just 11 percent had begun in August 1815 and none had begun in May 1815. Their government experience was also of recent origin—90 percent had held a post in the 1820s, only 47 percent in the Second Restoration. Their experience in the other periods followed the typical pattern for the Right of the Restoration. Also, as expected, most came from the West, 32 percent, and the South, 25 percent.

As part of the revisions of the Charter during the aftermath of the July days, the double vote was eliminated and the age requirements were lowered to 30 years for eligibility and 25 years for voting. Both the single-member and departmental constituencies were maintained, but all the voters could now participate in both elections. Further changes in the electoral system were delayed until the Chamber was brought to full strength. The by-elections took place in October 1830.

[2] Patrick B. and Trevor B. Higonnet, "Class Corruption and Politics in the French Chamber of Deputies, 1846–1848," *French Historical Studies* 5 (Fall 1967). I am not sure about the exact magnitude of the changes after 1834, since the authors never give precise figures for the whole Chamber nor do they provide the number of deputies in each party so one could calculate figures for the whole group.

The voter turnout for these by-elections was quite low. The Legitimists, as the remnants of the Right of the Restoration were called, refused to take the oath of allegiance to Louis-Philippe, and thus they were denied the vote. The Left won nearly all of the seats, and it especially won where less than half of the registered voters participated. The Left won 28 percent of its seats in such elections compared to none for the Right. Those voters who did vote were in favor of the Left—40 percent of the Left deputies and none of the Right deputies received over three-fourths of the votes cast. The voter who favored the Right had clearly stayed home in October 1830, but the mandates of those elected were at least as good as those of the early Restoration.

The men elected in October were vastly different from the resignees. For one thing, the new age requirements had a great effect—29 percent of those elected in October 1830 were under 40 years old. Young men were favored generally; only 9 percent were over 60 (see fig. 17). The new generation was gaining entrance into the new regime.

The social composition and experience of the deputies reflected the fact that the Left won 90 percent of the seats (see figs. 18–21). The men of October were 44 percent Bourgeois, only 13 percent Titled nobles. Their occupational distribution was fairly even with Law and Proprietor equal at 23 percent. These men were novices in politics, 79 percent of them were being elected for the first time, and even those who had held a government post previously were few. Forty percent had held

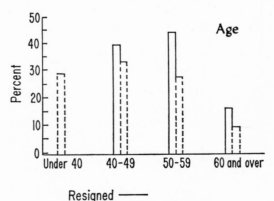

Resigned ———
Elected October 1830 - - - - -

Fig. 17.   October election.

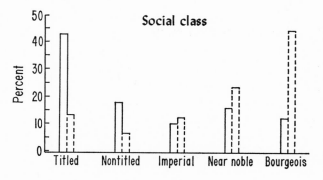

Resigned ————
Elected October 1830 ————

Fig. 18.   October election.

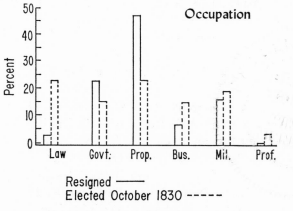

Resigned ————
Elected October 1830 ————

Fig. 19.   October election.

a post during the Napoleonic period, which was the largest amount for any period prior to the July Monarchy. What little experience they did have was oriented in the manner traditional for the Left. Seventeen percent had experience of the Revolution to only 4 percent who had emigrated. Also there was a 3 to 1 ratio in favor of Napoleon's return in 1815. These men had been nearly shut out of the Restoration; only 18 percent had held a post in the 1820s.[3] There was no unwillingness to hold a government post, if given the chance, since 64 percent would hold one

[3] Although 18 percent might seem like a large amount, it is relatively small compared to other groups of deputies. One must remember that

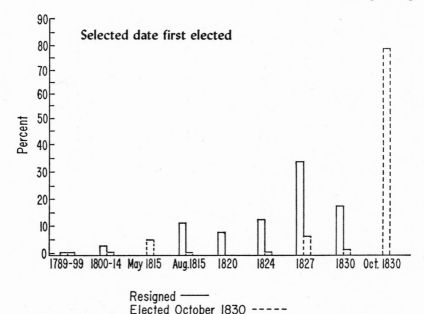

Fig. 20.   October election.

during the July Monarchy. Finally, these men who took immediate advantage of the July Revolution had neither great status,
only 34 percent had an Honor (see fig. 22), nor wealth, only 41
percent paid at least 1,500 francs in direct taxes.

The Marquis de Vaulchier and Béraud des Rondard, who has
already been discussed, both left the Chamber in August 1830.
They were replaced by Baron Désiré-Gilbert Bachelu and
Pierre-Hippolyte Raynaud respectively. Bachelu, born in 1777,
had served in the army from 1795 until Waterloo, where he was
wounded. He was a Baron of the Empire. After his election in
October 1830, Bachelu supported the Dynastic Opposition faction of the Left. Raynaud, on the other hand, was young, only
35 years old, an *avocat* by profession, and had no previous experience in the government. He supported the government in
the Chamber. Both of these men were being elected for the
first time, whereas those they replaced had long legislative and
governmental experience.

---

men on the Left usually served only during the brief periods of Center-
Left coalitions in 1817–1819 and 1828–1829.

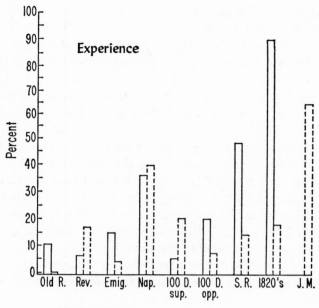

Fig. 21. October election.

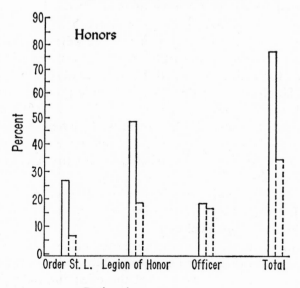

Fig. 22. October election.

An example of a man elected in October who had previous experience would be Jean-Jacques Duboys. Born in 1768, an *avocat* prior to the Revolution, he enlisted in the army in 1791. Soon raised to an officer, he served until 1797 when he began a career as a teacher of law at the Ecole Centrale of Maine-et-Loire. During the Empire Duboys served as assistant prosecutor-general from 1811 to 1814. Elected to the Chamber of Representatives from Maine-et-Loire he was revoked from his post in the magistrature at the Second Restoration. Heading the opposition in his department during the Restoration, he was defeated in the elections of June 1830, but he was elected a colonel in the National Guard of Angers in August 1830. Also, he regained his post in the magistrature as a prosecutor-general and was elected deputy in October 1830 and each election thereafter until 1839 as a supporter of the government.

By comparing the men who resigned or were excluded in 1830 with those elected to replace them, it is obvious something fundamental had changed because of the revolution of July. I examine these changes from the position of the electoral laws, regionalism, and politics later in this chapter, but before I undertake those analyses it is necessary to discuss the changes that continued to occur in the type of man elected in the first and second general elections of the July Monarchy.

In April 1831 the Chamber passed the new electoral law. It lowered the *cens* requirement to 500 francs for eligibility and to 200 francs for voting, increased the number of seats to 459, made them all single-member districts, and made the president of the electoral college an elected position. In June 1831 the new electorate had its first opportunity to employ the new law. One hundred ninety-six deputies of the Chamber were not re-elected and 191 men were first-time elected in this first election of the July Monarchy.

The evolution, which had begun in July 1830, was continued in the election of 1831 as the new voters elected a new generation of deputies. The problem of gerontocracy was being solved: 32 percent of those eliminated were over 60 years old compared to just 11 percent of those beginning. The youth movement was also continuing—only 6 percent of those leaving were under 40, whereas 34 percent of the new men were under 40 (see fig. 23).

The new generation was not only young, it was of a different

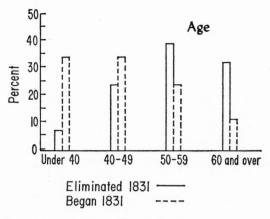

Eliminated 1831 ——
Began 1831 ----

Fig. 23.   June election.

social composition. The disenchantment with the traditional elite was accelerated. Twenty-six percent of those eliminated were Titled compared to just 4 percent of the new men. Not only were men with Old Regime titles in disfavor, but so were all men with high social standing, when that standing is measured in the old legal manner. The Nontitled nobles were 12 percent of those eliminated but just 3 percent of the new men. The Imperial nobles maintained themselves slightly better than those with Old Regime heritage, yet even the Imperial nobles were 15 percent of those leaving and only 5 percent of those entering. The Bourgeois, on the other hand, were 27 percent of those eliminated but 64 percent of those beginning (see fig. 24). The Revolution of 1789 may have ended the old legal classes, but it took the Revolution of 1830 before these classes stopped having great political power.

The occupational categories also reflected a new distribution. The men not re-elected were 33 percent Proprietors and 11 percent Law; the new men were only 20 percent Proprietors and 27 percent Law. The Professions also showed a marked increase from 3 percent to 12 percent (see fig. 25). The traditional elites were being eliminated in favor of men who had earned their position in the New France. The increase in the Law and Professions was partially a result of the lower *cens* requirements and partially a result of a change in the voter's preference. The voters appeared ready to entrust their government to men who

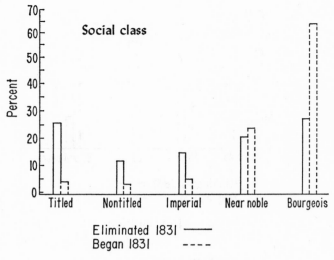

Fig. 24. June election.

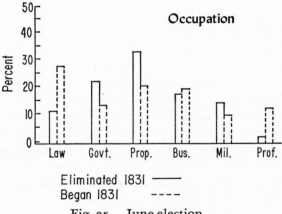

Fig. 25. June election.

had more active occupations and even the Legitimists turned to such men with more frequency after 1830.

The men eliminated in 1831 were not just men on the Right, despite their social composition; in fact, 58 percent were on the Left, but many of these were from the moderate Left of 1827–1830. The overall experience of these men reflected this orientation and reflected their old age (see fig. 26). This greater age inflated the number who had served in the pre-Restoration peri-

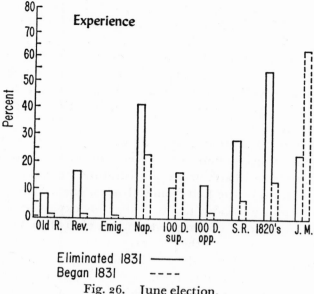

Eliminated 1831 ————
Began 1831 — — — —

Fig. 26. June election.

ods when compared to the young men beginning in 1831, and the Left orientation established the relationship among the types of experience. The men leaving had 16 percent who had held a post during the Revolution to 9 percent who had been émigrés. The new men had 5 percent who had held a post and 1 percent who had been émigrés. The moderate nature of those being eliminated can be seen in their experience of the One Hundred Days, where 11 percent had held a post and 12 percent had opposed Napoleon's return; for the new men, 16 percent had held a post and only 2 percent had opposed Napoleon.

The retiring deputies had served Napoleon during the Empire, since 41 percent had held a post, but they had been most firmly attached to the Restoration, especially toward its end. Fifty-four percent had held a post in the 1820s and 38 percent had begun their legislative careers in either 1827 or 1830. Also, the last remnants of the generation of the Second Restoration were being eliminated, since 10 percent had been first-time elected in August 1815, which would leave only 1 percent of the total Chamber of 1831 who began their careers in August 1815.

The new deputies had an antipathy toward the Restoration, which was visible in their pattern of experience. Only 6 percent

had held a post during the Second Restoration and only 13 percent had held one during the 1820s. This extremely low level
of office-holding was not a matter of choice, however. Even
though most had been too young to have held a post under the
Empire, 22 percent had and 65 percent were also to hold a post
during the July Monarchy. This was a new generation, which
had not been allowed the benefits of the political system under
the Restoration.

Some typical representatives of this new generation were
Guillaume-François Thouret—49 years old, the son of a Constituent, who had been in the magistrature from 1811 to 1814
and was elected by the Left from Calvados, Marie-Stanislas Bres-
son—born to a Girondin the year after his expulsion from the
Convention, who was a Proprietor when elected in Vosges and
was one made eligible by the lower *cens* requirement, and finally,
Leonard-Joseph Havin—whose father was a regicide and member
of the Council of Ancients. Born in 1799, Havin emigrated with
his father in 1816–1820 and upon his return to Caen he led the
young liberals. A justice of the peace in 1830 he sat with the
Dynastic Opposition faction of the Left in the Chamber.

In 1831 the areas of France that were making the most rapid
adjustment to the new order were the Central Mountains and
the South. Nationally, the new men represented 42 percent of
the total Chamber, but in the Central Mountains 76 percent
of its deputies were first-time elected, and in the South 52 percent were new men. The South was making its second adjustment; it and the West had had many deputies replaced in the
October 1830 by-elections.

Besides the fact that nearly all of the Right of the Restoration
and a good share of the Left of the Restoration were eliminated, there was a switching of party affiliation in 1831. Of
course, this change did not take place in 1831 but when the
July Revolution occurred. Because of the logistics of handling the deputies, I did not re-label the party affiliations of the
deputies until the elections of 1831. This allowed me to compare
the Chamber of 1830 to the other Restoration Chambers. When
the change was made, those on the Left of the Restoration tended
to move to the Right of the July Monarchy. Of the 143 deputies
on the Left in 1827 who were re-elected in 1831, 67 percent were
on the Right in 1831, and of the 163 deputies on the Left in

June 1830 who were re-elected in 1831, 71 percent were on the Right in 1831. Finally, of the 69 men on the Left in October 1830 who were re-elected in 1831, 75 percent were on the Right. Only 7 men in June 1830 and 5 men in October 1830 who were on the Right or Extreme Right were re-elected in June 1831. Here was a clear indication of political influence on the type of deputies elected: men who switched positions on the political spectrum. More accurately, the political spectrum was shifted to the left by the revolution of July and the men remained stationary.

The movement toward a bourgeois deputy with an orientation to the New France was thus furthered in 1831. The dramatic change in the type of man elected could have been caused by the new electoral law. In order to evaluate this possibility, I analyze the problem from two angles: by comparing the men elected in October 1830 under the old *cens* requirements to the men elected in June 1831 under the new ones, and by comparing the changes in the composition of the electorate to the changes in the composition of the deputies.

At first glance the men elected in October 1830 appear to offer a good sample by which to evaluate the legal changes made under the July Monarchy. They were elected under the old requirements, but after the revolution of July. The political climate was of the July Monarchy, but the electoral system was that of the Restoration. Also, since there were only eight months separating this election from the first election of the July Monarchy, we may assume that these elections were held under similar economic conditions. However, the changes in the Charter had lowered the age requirements for the October by-elections, so that it is really only the effect of the *cens* requirement that is being analyzed here. Those elected in October 1830 had to pay at least 1,000 francs in direct taxes and were elected by men paying at least 300 francs; those elected in June 1831 had to pay only 500 francs and were elected by men paying at least 200 francs.

The lowering of the age requirements made a radical difference—29 percent of those elected in October were under 40. A further 33 percent were in their forties and a mere 9 percent were over 60 years old. This made these men younger than those elected in June 1831. However, I have not found a correlation between age and social class or occupation. Therefore, the lower age of the October deputies should not affect the evaluation of the change in *cens* required between the October 1830 group and the June 1831 group in these two categories.

The influence of the *cens* requirements on the social class and occupation of the deputies appears to be minimal. The October deputies were 19 percent Old Regime nobles, 12 percent Imperial nobles, and 44 percent Bourgeois; the June deputies were 14 percent Old Regime nobles, 13 percent Imperial nobles, and 49 percent Bourgeois. The same close relationship was true for the occupational distribution, where the October deputies were 23 percent Proprietors and 23 percent Law, and the June deputies were 24 percent Proprietors and 21 percent Law. It seemed that the noble or Proprietor deputy of the Restoration was not a product of the electoral law since there was little change from the October 1830 to the June 1831 election.

The experience of the deputies was also not affected by the new law. Most of the men elected in October, 79 percent, were being first-time elected, but the 5 percent who began their careers in May 1815 and the 7 percent who began in 1827 were the only groups from any single election with over 4 percent. The June 1831 deputies had only 41 percent who were first-time elected, but again the One Hundred Days was the only major beginning point prior to 1827. The nonlegislative experience also was very similar for the two groups.

Although the new law did not cause the shift in the type of man elected in terms of his occupation and social class, it did, like the change in the age requirements, introduce a new element into the Chamber—those paying less than 1,000 francs comprised 7 percent of the deputies elected in October and 27 percent of those elected in June 1831. Those elected in October were actually in violation of the law of the Restoration, but in the atmosphere of the new regime this was not strictly adhered to. Despite this change both groups had about 60 percent who paid below 1,500 francs and about 5 percent who paid above 5,000 francs, so this addition of low taxpaying deputies caused little change in the percentage of the highest taxpaying deputies, but it did reduce those who paid a moderate tax.

The lowering of the *cens* requirements under the July Monarchy, therefore, appears to have had little influence on the type of man elected outside of the categories affected by the change in the requirements, age and the under-1,000-franc taxpayer. In

the two categories most closely associated with the *cens* requirements, social class and occupation, there was little difference between the two groups. The change in the electoral law was not
what made the voters of the July Monarchy choose a deputy who
was bourgeois and oriented toward the New France. This can be
further demonstrated by examining the changes in the electorate.

By comparing the change in the composition of the electorate
from the Restoration to the July Monarchy with the change in
the composition of the deputies at the end of the Restoration and
the beginning of the July Monarchy, the effect of the legal change
can be evaluated from another perspective. A full analysis of the
electorate has not been done, but Sherman Kent has provided a
distribution of those eligible for office and those who could vote
in 1829.[4] By extrapolating these figures it is possible to estimate
the occupations of those eligible and those who could vote under
the requirements of the July Monarchy. The results are in
percent:

Occupations	Eligibles		Electorate		
	(Rest.) 1,000	(July M.) 500	(Rest.) 300	(July M.) 200	*Cens* required
Government	23	20	17	15	
Professional	4	4	5	10	
Business	11	16	19	20	
Landed	62	60	59	55	

These figures can be used in two ways: the change in those eligible for office, from the 1,000 to 500 *cens*, versus the change in
those deputies elected, and the change in those who could vote,
from the 300 to the 200 *cens*, versus the change in those deputies
elected. In order to try to reduce any one-time quirks, I have
used the results of 1827 and 1830 to represent the Restoration
and results of 1831 and 1834 to represent the July Monarchy.

Comparing the percent change in the eligibles with the percent change in the deputies yields the following figures (in percent):[5]

---

[4] Sherman Kent, *Electoral Procedures under Louis-Philippe* (New Haven,
1937), pp. 10n, 13n.

[5] I have adapted my occupational groupings to those of Kent according
to: Government equals Government, Professional equals Law plus Professions, Business equals Business, and Landed equals Proprietor plus Military.

Occupations	Eligibles	Deputies
Government	−13	−23
Professional	0	162
Business	46	۹
Landed	−3	−25

The changes in those eligible do not explain the changes in the type of deputies elected, even though the direction of all changes is the same. The oddity is among the Business deputies. The July Monarchy was supposed to be the businessman's regime, but his share of the deputies did not keep pace with his increased share of the eligibles. This may indicate that businessmen under the July Monarchy were more satisfied to have men of different occupations represent them than under the Restoration. Of course nothing definite can be said, because the businessmen did not vote as a block, nor were they a homogeneous group. Nevertheless, although there were many more businessmen eligible to run for office under the July Monarchy, few more did so successfully.

A comparison of the change in the electorate with that in the deputies provides a better explanation of the changes between the two regimes than a comparison of those eligible to run for office (in percent):

Occupations.	Electorate	Deputies
Government	−12	−23
Professional[6]	100	162
Business	5	3
Landed	−7	−25

Here the changes are not only in the same direction, but their magnitudes are much closer. The new generation of deputies was younger, more often engaged in the active occupations, and was looking to advance according to individual talent. The traditional elites, whose positions were based on heredity and land and who had dominated the Restoration, could not maintain that dominance with the expanded electorate. This truth, however, cannot be discerned from the occupational breakdown of

---

[6] The estimate for this group of the electorate was the most difficult, and I may have overestimated it. The percent change, therefore, may have been somewhat less than 100 percent.

the electorate. For that it is necessary to seek a political change, not a legal one.

The political change of the July Monarchy worked a revolution in the type of man elected. The new laws allowed the new generation to come of age all at once, but the shift in political opinion was not just a consequence of age. The Restoration had appeared to be a period of conflict between the Revolution and the Old Regime, with members of the traditional elite favored as deputies, especially on the Right, but I believe only the fear of disorder allowed the traditional elite a chance to rule. When the acceptance of the basic value of constitutionalism and enough freedom to make representative government a reality was challenged and once the Left adopted a lawful and more conservative appearance it succeeded with the electorate. Thus when Charles X forced the situation, the revolution was successful and the acceptance of the Revolution was assured. The conflict then could become what it had long been: one of how far the Revolution should continue and not one of its basic acceptance. In this clarified situation the voter chose the men of the New France to debate the problems of the New France. The traditional elite had had its chance to lead and had failed; it would take some years for these men to accept the situation, and then only some of them would regain their positions of leadership. During the Restoration the roads to positions of power had been blocked off to many talented men and these men had not participated in the Restoration. With the July Revolution this type of man found his opportunity and he seized it. That the new generation also was to fail to move with progress would be the story of 1848.

The changes brought by the Revolution of 1830 had a great effect not only on the type of deputy elected generally, but also on the distribution between the parties. I have already explained how it became necessary to change the party labels for many men. The Right of the Restoration had been virtually eliminated, leaving behind only the factional Legitimist group. The new Right was now the government party and also occupied the conservative position. Its members' profiles show the shift in the political spectrum as well as the move forward into the nineteenth century.

The new Right won over 60 percent of the seats in 1831 and

1834. The men of the new Right were young, but an old guard did exist. Fifty-one percent were under 50 years old, a figure nearly equal to the Right that began the Restoration, but 18 percent of the Right of 1831 were over 60 years old. These old men were primarily men from the Left of the Restoration who had achieved their goal and who now took a more conservative position.

The social composition and experience of the new Right was quite similar to the Left of 1827–1830. The Bourgeois dominated with 50 percent, for the Old Regime noble did not find a haven on the new Right—he comprised only 14 percent in 1831 and just 19 percent in 1834. Occupation showed a like change; Proprietors dropped dramatically while Law and Business rose. The result for the Right of 1831 and 1834 was near equality among these categories. The men of the New France had fought the Restoration and won; the July Monarchy was to be theirs. The Business deputy had been only 7 percent of the Right in 1830, but this type of deputy moved into the new Right, where he occupied 24 percent in 1831.

The new Right had its origins in the Left of 1827–1830, but it also added a substantial portion of its members during the first two elections of the July Monarchy. Eighty-two percent of the Right of 1831 had begun their legislative careers in the elections of 1827 or later. Its youth prevented many from having experienced government service before 1815, yet for those who had there was a strong bias in favor of the Revolution. Fourteen percent had held a post during the Revolution, whereas just 1 percent had been émigrés. There was also a 6 to 1 ratio in support of the return of Napoleon: the largest amount of experience came during the Napoleonic period, when 35 percent had held a post.

The Restoration had been a period when the men of the new Right had not held a government post with any frequency. Thirteen percent had served in the Second Restoration and 30 percent had held a post in the 1820s, but many of the positions in the latter period were held during the brief interlude of Martignac's ministry. The periods where the government was consistently friendly to the type of men who sat on the Right of the July Monarchy came mostly before the return of the Bourbons and after their demise.

Although the new Right was a radical departure from the Right of the Restoration, the new Left was not very different from the Left of the Restoration. The July Revolution had amputated the right of the political spectrum; it had not yet created an extension on the left of any great proportions. The new Left, which was moderately successful in its opposition in 1831 and 1834, winning about 35 percent of the seats each time, had some carry-over from the old Left, but it was basically composed of both new and young men. The youth of the party was greater than the new Right's in 1831 and this difference increased in 1834. In that year 62 percent of the Left were under 50 years old and only 13 percent were over 60. The legislative experience of the new Left deputies was commensurate with their age— only 13 percent had begun their careers before 1827 and 79 percent had begun after the July Revolution.

The men of the Left of the July Monarchy were more bourgeois than during the Restoration, with more in the professional occupations. The Bourgeois category comprised 36 percent of the old Left in 1830 and 53 percent of the new Left in 1831. The rise in this category also affected the occupations. There were 11 percent in Law and 2 percent in Professions in 1830, but 28 percent and 14 percent respectively in these occupations in 1831. Business declined on the Left from 27 percent to 12 percent at the same time; this latter type of deputy had switched to the Right. The occupational distribution of the new Left, however, was not dominated by any one category, as Law had dominated among the members of the Corps Législatif. The New France had won a great victory, but it was a victory based on compromise. Not even the opposition had the more radical profile of the pre-Restoration legislators.

The men who did want to carry the Revolution of 1830 further were not only bourgeois and young, but generally they had little experience. Although their experience had the same orientation as that of the new Right, since both favored the Revolution and had a strong attachment to the Empire, it was less in every period. The new Left had its greatest amount of pre– July Monarchy experience under Napoleon, 34 percent, but under the July Monarchy itself 62 percent held a post. This figure was higher than one might expect because some of these men held a post in the early days of the regime before the new opposi-

tion developed and others held a post in the local administration—
many local posts became elective early in the new regime.[7]

The two parties were not very different in the type of men
they elected in 1831 and 1834. The total membership of the
Chamber elected in 1834 can therefore serve as a good summary for the type of man elected by the early period of the
July Monarchy, when the new generation had taken control. By
this second election of the new regime the boycotting by the
Legitimists had ended, although the overall voter participation
was only equal to that of 1831;[8] the participation appeared to
level off at about 60 percent after the high turnouts of 1827 and
1830 (see fig. 27). By 1834 the Right was winning more seats, but
it was also having its level of support reduced, since it had more
members win with a bare majority. In general there seemed to be
more competition in 1834; both parties had a sharp decline in

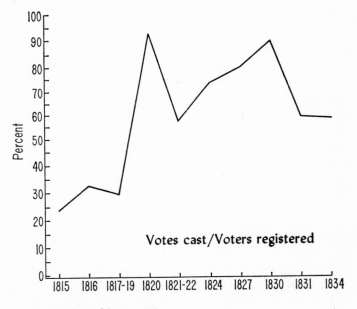

Districts with over 75 percent ———

Fig. 27.   Voter participation.

[7] André-Jean Tudesq, *Les conseillers généraux en France au temps de
Guizot, 1840–1848* (Paris, 1967), pp. 21–77.

[8] The equal participation in the two elections leads me to think that
the amount of Legitimist abstentions has been exaggerated.

those who received over half of the registered electorate's vote despite the turnout equal to that of 1831.

The expanded electorate had elected a new generation of men to the Chamber. In 1834, 57 percent of the deputies were under 50 years old and 64 percent had begun their legislative careers after the July Revolution. At the other end of the scale, only 15 percent were over 60 years old and only 14 percent had begun their careers before 1827. The youth of 1834 was most dramatically demonstrated by the fact that 38 percent of the deputies had not been born until after the Revolution of 1789.

The Old France, with its traditional elite, was gone. Only 13 percent of the deputies had Old Regime titles, and 45 percent were in the Bourgeois category. The occupations reflected a cross section of the categories. Law was largest at 23 percent, Business had 17 percent, Proprietors 22 percent, and Professions 7 percent. The lower *cens* requirements helped increase the number in the Bourgeois and in the active occupations. The taxes paid were lower—35 percent now paid less than 1,000 francs and only 39 percent paid at least 1,500 francs.[9]

The new generation of deputies had seldom served the Restoration and many were too young to have served before the Restoration. Just 10 percent had held a post during the Revolution; the men of that generation were being eliminated. The Napoleonic period, however, was a fertile one for these men; 36 percent held a post then, but when Napoleon fell so did they. Many remained loyal to Napoleon when he returned: 17 percent held a post to 6 percent who opposed his return. They did

[9] For those who have read Patrick Higonnet, "La composition de la Chambre de Députés de 1827 à 1831," *Revue historique* 239 (April–June 1968), you will notice the differences in my figures for 1831 are substantial. Higonnet understates the nobles, overstates the lawyers, and as in his other work on the deputies of 1846–1848 his presentation makes it difficult to compare figures. We have other disagreements on the figures and at times they are substantial, especially on the Chamber of 1815. Although I feel Higonnet understates the nobles in 1831 and overstates them in 1846, we do agree on several of the basic changes that occur in 1830. I, however, cannot accept his strong economic determinism in assessing the chances for new directions at the beginning of the July Monarchy, especially since the elections of 1834 do not show an early end to the opportunities that Higonnet finds in the results of 1831, which he implies ended soon thereafter.

not enjoy the benefits of office during the Restoration; only 14 percent held a post during the Second Restoration and 28 percent held one during the 1820s. This latter figure might appear significant, but considered against the one for the July Monarchy when 70 percent had held a post it is not. The deputies of the July Monarchy had not found the Restoration conducive to beginning a career, nor did many maintain one begun under Napoleon. For example, François-Gabriel Vallée, a deputy of Sarthe, had served in the magistrature in the last years of the Empire; but he engaged in agriculture during the Restoration and only regained his government position after the July Revolution.

In trying to explain why this new generation of deputies appeared, I have already eliminated the electoral laws as a fundamental cause and stated that the political atmosphere fostered the change. Now I want to once again use the regional and social-economic-demographic analysis to see if the political changes can be better explained.

Just as the social differences between the deputies of the two parties disappeared in the July Monarchy, so did the SED correlations with the political parties—there were no significant correlations with either the Left or the Right in the elections of 1831 or 1834. The political changes had thus eliminated the relationships that had been present in 1827 and 1830 and also ended the regional distribution of the parties which had existed during the Restoration.

The regionalism of the July Monarchy was a new one, and it varied only slightly between 1831 and 1834 (see maps 14 and 15).[10] In 1831 a region that supported the Left did so for one of two reasons: it favored the Left or it opposed the government. The Lower West fell into the first category; it voted with the Left in both 1831 and 1834. The South fell into the second category; it voted with the Left in 1831, but it gave the Legitimists heavy support in 1834. Two other regions, the West and Channel, supported the Left in 1834 after voting at the national average in 1831.

The Left did not have great support in any one region. Only the Lower West had more than half of its deputies on the Left

10 And see the percentages in table 17, Appendix C.

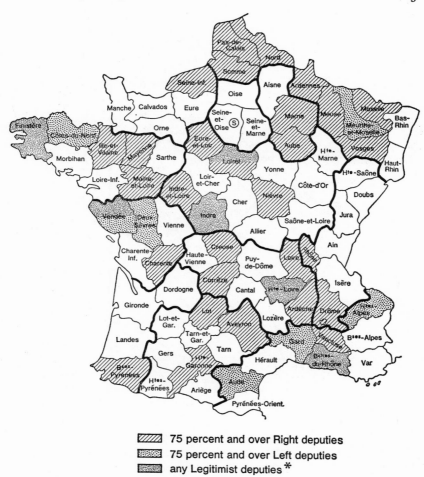

```
▨▨▨  75 percent and over Right deputies
▒▒▒  75 percent and over Left deputies
▨▨▨  any Legitimist deputies *
```

* The Legitimists are excluded from the calculations for the percent of the Left and the Right in each departmental delegation.

Map 14.   Elections of 1831, by department.

in both elections, and this region had long opposed the government. In 1817 to 1822 it had voted with the left and in 1824 to
1830 it had given a large vote to the Extreme Right. This latter
type of vote did not persist into the July Monarchy, however,
since no Legitimists were elected in the Lower West in 1834.

The Right had new regions of support under the July Monarchy, for the southern third of the country was no longer solidly
behind the Right. The South region, itself, maintained some

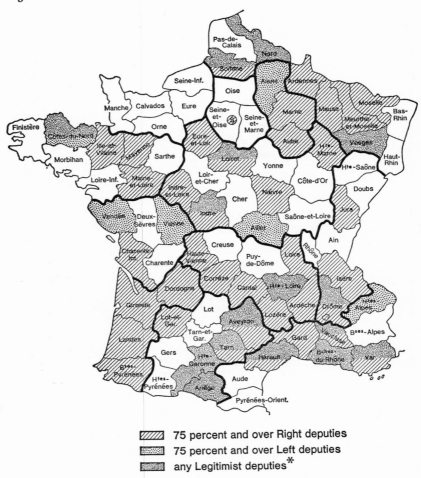

75 percent and over Right deputies
75 percent and over Left deputies
any Legitimist deputies*

* See note to map 14.

Map 15.   Elections of 1834, by department.

support of the Right of the Restoration, the Legitimists, but it
fell short of the national average for the new Right; Aquitaine
did the same thing in 1834. The traditional Right regions of
the Central Mountains and the South Coast, however, did support the new Right in 1834. The new areas that supported the
Right were the old bastions of the Left, the East and Champagne
and the Paris Area, which had been a strong supporter of the
Left of the late Restoration. The shift of these last three areas
should not surprise us, since we know that the old Left and the

new Right had much in common. However, these were not the only regions to support the new Right; the North also was well above the national average in this regard.

No particular factor seems to account for the party distribution of the new regime. Geography offers no clue on either the social-economic-demographic or the traditional provinces bases. There was some continuance of the old Left regions for the new Right, but there was also continuance between some old Right regions and the new Right and between some old Left regions and the new Left.

The July Revolution was an important watershed in French history. The Restoration had failed, and with it the traditional elite's attempt at ruling the New France. The old ruling elite was greatly reduced in 1830–1831 and the new ruling elite, which was based on the nineteenth-century society, was given power. The new generation was not composed of men of the Revolution; these men had composed the Left of the Restoration and had made the Revolution of 1830, but they were quickly replaced by the post-Revolution generation. The new men had close connections to the Napoleonic period; although they did not necessarily favor its leader or its military glory, they did find it a period where men of talent could have a place. The generation of the early July Monarchy had often begun their careers during the Empire, but they had been shut out when the Bourbons returned. When the Restoration alienated the wealthy and more advanced areas of France the Revolution of 1830 came, and for the moment the old sore was healed as the men of the New France took over once again. There would be a few years of adjusting to the new developments, but the Old France was gone; progress would continue and another "New France" would evolve under the July Monarchy. As under the Restoration, maneuvering the electoral laws would not prevent this development.

X

CONCLUSION

In this study I have not dealt with the question of whose interests were represented in the Chamber, even though this critical question must be answered before any final conclusions can be drawn. I chose to avoid the decisions taken by the Chamber because no basic disagreement existed among the ruling group on the important questions of economics. It was not until 1827 that even a small group, which advocated free trade, formed in the Chamber. Throughout the period in which I am studying the deputies, the issues of capitalism and industrialization did not divide the ruling classes.[1] The emotional issues for the society of this period dealt with political questions: electoral laws and press restrictions were the types of decisions which clearly divided the deputies into two groups, as were the issues that remained from the Revolution. After the Revolution of 1830 the area of economic issues would become more important, but not until the 1840s would the question of economic democracy become a divisive force among the ruling classes. I also avoided dealing with the decisions of the Chamber because the votes of the deputies were secret. I wanted to study all of the deputies, not just the men who were important enough to speak on an issue or to have their vote noted in the press. Therefore, I chose to study only the group characteristics of the deputies.

The Revolution of 1830 remains a convenient pivot in this

[1] S. Charléty, *La Restauration* (Paris, 1921), pp. 271–272; G. Bertier de Sauvigny, *The Bourbon Restoration* (Philadelphia, 1966), pp. 223–238; and Jean Vidalenc, *La société française de 1815 à 1848: Le peuple des campagnes* (Paris, 1970).

period of French history. There was a basic transformation that occurred at that time and it effected more than just the change in personnel that David Pinkney has claimed.[2] Pinkney identified a resurgence of Napoleonic men after the Revolution of 1830; this cannot be disputed.[3] However, I do have to offer a few modifications on the type of resurgence. The Revolution of 1830 did not allow a return of the Napoleonic noble, since he had never really left the scene, and his small position in the Chamber was not enhanced by the revolution. The actual number of men who held posts under the Empire also decreased after 1830, but beneath these raw figures the fundamental truth of Pinkney's argument is evident because after the July Revolution a new generation of politicians emerged who had strong connections to the Napoleonic period. These men were young; about one-third of the deputies elected in 1831 and in 1834 had been under 20 years old when Napoleon fell from power. They had not had the opportunity to serve the Emperor, which I believe they would have done if time had allowed, since the older men elected in these years had served Napoleon. More important than the experience of the Empire, however, is the fact that such a large portion of the deputies elected in 1831–1834 had a lack of involvement in the Restoration (see fig. 28). From 1815 to 1830 many future deputies just had not been in government service. It took the Revolution of 1830 to destroy the roadblocks to public office created by the Restoration, especially to offices they would have enjoyed under Napoleon. Thus the Napoleonic resurgence was not so much a return of men who actually had held office under the Emperor as it was an emergence of young men who had looked forward to holding office under him.

Even the change in personnel, however, was based on a more fundamental political change than Pinkney identifies. Although I have shown the electoral laws to have been unimportant in changing the ratio of occupations of the electorate to those of the deputies, this did not mean the laws had no effect. The new electoral laws of the July Monarchy admitted two new strata of society into political power, this doubled the number of Business and Professions people in the electorate, and by lowering the

[2] David H. Pinkney, *The French Revolution of 1830* (Princeton, 1972), p. 276.
[3] Ibid., pp. 289–295.

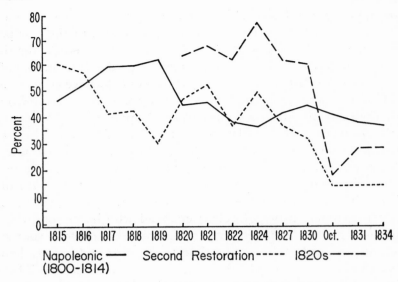

Fig. 28. Deputies: Government Experience.

age limit allowed an entire generation of voters into power at one time. Because of this, profound change occurred. The very fact that nearly three-fourths of the Left moved to the Right after the July Revolution is significant. Certainly this statistic occurred because of my definitions, but recall that my definitions were derived from the contemporary ones. I did not create the political spectrum shift in 1830; I only recorded the movement. Such a movement was much more than a change in personnel.

In the realm of social distinctions, the Revolution of 1830 also marked a watershed. Unlike the political one, the social change was artificial. That is, I have chosen the political event of a revolution to decree that a social change had occurred, when in reality it had been evolving over a period of years. However, I feel using the July Revolution as the dividing point is justified because contemporaries did the same thing. This was the origin of the label for the July Monarchy of the "bourgeois monarchy."

If the old legal definitions of social class are employed, as I employed them in my category of Social class, then the Revolution of 1830 did inaugurate the bourgeois monarchy (see fig 29). The Old Regime nobles were greatly reduced and the Bourgeois, those without even a pretense to noble status, dominated in the Chamber. Of course, this did not represent either social or po-

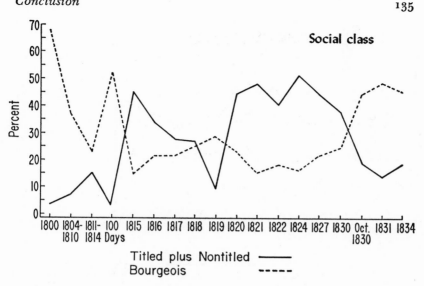

Fig. 29. Deputies: Noble vs. Bourgeois.

litical reality. The legal classes had disappeared in 1789, but the old habits could not be erased overnight. I think the distinction between noble and roturier was important during the Restoration, and apparently the voters also thought so (see fig. 30). One fact I do not know, which would only add support to my thesis, was whether the voters also divided themselves on these same lines. That is, were the Left voters more bourgeois and the Right voters more noble? In any case, after the Revolution of 1830 the old division was gone. The tradition of classes based on heredity was finally laid to rest. The noble deputy was reduced to a position that was much closer to his share of the population, and the parties were no longer divided by these class distinctions even though class divisions did not end in 1830 nor did noble status become unimportant. This was why contemporaries described the July Monarchy as the bourgeois monarchy: the Third Estate was now in command. This again was more than a change in personnel, since the Chamber began to reflect the social realities of the New France.

Pinkney misses this fundamental point about the social distinctions. He says:

> After the Revolution [of 1830] the landed proprietor, the
> official class, and the professional men continued to pre-

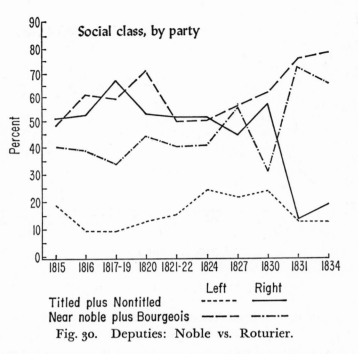

Fig. 30. Deputies: Noble vs. Roturier.

dominate in the key offices of state as they had under the
Empire and the Bourbon Restoration. Here the Revolution
had introduced no new regime of the *grande bourgeoisie*.[4]

For Pinkney to lump together all occupations except business
and then to say this group dominated is to say the obvious in
light of the lack of French industrialization. This absence of
development, which only recently is receiving proper attention
from historians, is crucial to a proper understanding of this
period, for you cannot equate businessmen and the bourgeoisie,
not even the *grande bourgeoisie*. This mixing of old social class
terminology with occupations only leads to confusion; just because Karl Marx did this, no excuse exists for a continuation of
the practice. The term bourgeois in the Marxist sense should not
be used in describing French society in the early nineteenth century; only confusion results from it.[5] The Marxist class was too
small for such a general term and of course the men of the 1830s

[4] Pinkney, *Revolution of 1830*, p. 275.

[5] Pinkney's search for bourgeois among the miltary and magistrature is a
case in point. See his *Revolution of 1830*, pp. 280–289.

did not think in those terms. By the 1830s the term began to have the same type of meaning that "aristocrat" had in the Great Revolution—that is, a convenient label for one's enemies. Thus, the use of the Old Regime definition is best and by 1830 even this must be abandoned. You can no more use an old concept in the new society than you can use Marx's term, which comes from a future society, in an earlier one. In this period the Business deputies were ironmasters, merchants, manufacturers, and bankers, and although these are all bourgeois, not all bourgeois are businessmen. Therefore, in this study bourgeois is used to describe only the legal Old Regime social class, and occupational groups were used to describe the New France. With these classifications a much different view of the period evolves than the one Pinkney presents, that the three regimes were similar in their types of personnel; this study clearly demonstrates that there were significant changes between each regime. The term "bourgeois" has no real utility after 1830, since the Old France was disappearing, and it was occupations, lifestyle, and wealth that became the determinants of social class in the New France. So the use of occupational groups is more appropriate than the Old Regime term "bourgeois."[6]

If occupations are used to define classes then a cross section of the upper part of society emerged among the deputies after 1830; there was no one dominant category, only an end to the preponderance of the Proprietor category. Proprietor had been the largest group under the Restoration, partly due to its close relationship with the nobility. After the July Revolution it remained a strong group, even though the nobility suffered a sharp decline (see fig. 31). The purely landed deputies were not eliminated by the Revolution of 1830, but neither were they enhanced —they no longer were dominant.

Business deputies also did not take over in 1830, although they did assume an important role in the government. What did change in 1830 was the political affiliation of many of these depu-

[6] This is not to claim that such groups had no internal conflicts, but some categorization is necessary if one is to explain the past. Those who subscribe to the Richard Cobb school of individualism like to believe they avoid categorizing their individuals, but it is impossible. Their warnings about overgeneralizing must be heeded, just as those about reading future groups into the past must be.

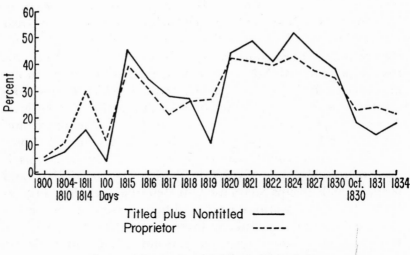

Fig. 31. Deputies: Noble vs. Proprietor.

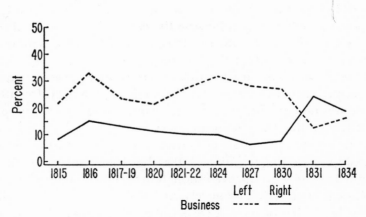

Fig. 32. Business deputies, by party.

ties, since under the Restoration the ratio of the percent of
Business deputies on the Left as compared to those on the Right
was about 3 to 1, but after the revolution of July it was 2 to 3
(see fig. 32). Without being able to offer any proof from this
study, I believe that this group's primary commitment was to
political policies and not business ones. They believed in the
Revolution because it gave them freedom. When Charles X
appeared to threaten the basic achievements of the Revolution,

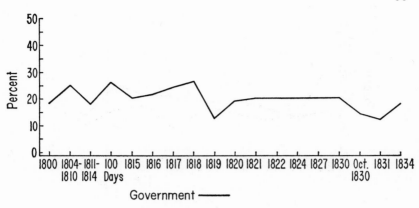

Fig. 33.   Government deputies.

they supported the opposition; after July 1830 they moved be-hind the government because their view of the Revolution had been accomplished. I think the development of capitalism or industrialization was incidental and that the Revolution of 1830 marked a political watershed, but this carried social over-tones just as the Revolution of 1789 had. The middle classes had been on the Left during the Restoration, opposed to the tradi-tional elites; under the July Monarchy new sides were being formed. The Business deputies were not clear as to which side they favored after 1830, but they leaned toward the Right, and they remained a strong group.

Government was another large occupational group and it held a strong position in all the regimes (see fig. 33), but the Govern-ment category is difficult to include in any analysis of who domi-nated because officeholders always gained their position from the current regime and their livelihood was dependent upon that regime. Since the officeholders had a constant and impor-tant voice in all the regimes, the important question here is why there were so many Government deputies. We know that the Government deputies tended to be elected from the poorer de-partments. I do not think this was because these departments had the fewest voters, thus enabling the voters and the deputies to be controlled by the government's purse strings; I do think that the lack of wealth was the key factor, because this meant there were few men eligible to run for office and these few dominated both the elective and appointive offices. Even though

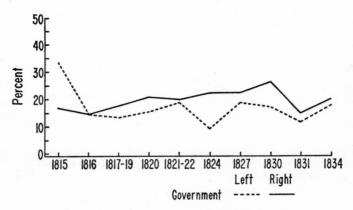

Fig. 34. Government deputies, by party.

the law made provisions for a minimum number of men to be
eligible by going below the required *cens* level, the additional
men were probably still incapable of running for office; being
a deputy required one to be in Paris for six months each year
and such an expense was beyond the means of men who paid
less than the required taxes.[7] Therefore the government was
forced to appoint the few men available regardless of their politics. Thus, even though the Right, the party that supported the
government, always had a greater share of the Government deputies, there were still a substantial number in the opposition parties (see fig. 34). This leads me to believe that my explanation
is correct, rather than the idea that the Government deputies
were the pawns of the government.[8]

The last major occupational group, the Law category, was
different from the Government category; Law was intimately
connected to the political tradition of favoring the Revolution.
This category was composed mostly of lawyers, and as any study
of legislators around the world will show there is a great affinity
between law and politics. It is often assumed that Law represents other groups in society and thus there would be more men
of this type in the Chamber than in the population in general.
This was true in my study, but this overrepresentation was much
greater in the periods associated with the Revolution. I think

[7] Louis Girard, *La Libéralisme en France de 1814 à 1848* (Paris, 1967),
p. 19.
[8] Girard, *La Libéralisme*, p. 20.

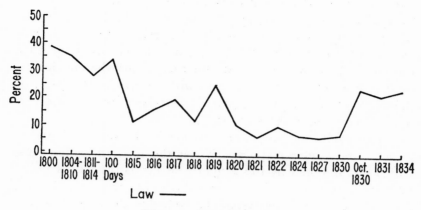

Fig. 35. Law deputies.

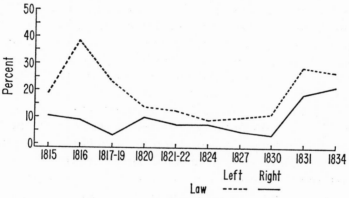

Fig. 36. Law deputies, by party.

that lawyers felt a particularly strong stake in the issues being debated and this caused them to enter politics. They had been prominent during the Revolution and this interest did not wane[9]—it associated them with the Napoleonic period, especially at its beginning, the One Hundred Days, the Left of the early Restoration, and the July Monarchy (see fig. 35).

Here again the Revolution of 1830 marked a change. The

[9] Alison Kary Houston Patrick, "The French National Convention of 1792–93: A Study of Political Alignments," (Melbourne, 1969). I want to thank Professor François Furet for allowing me to read this work before its recent publication.

Law deputies increased greatly after the July days and they were now found on the Right as well as on the Left in significant numbers (see fig. 36). I believe they represented themselves and their belief in political freedom, and only incidentally other interests. The Law category had fluctuated with the political issues; its identification was always with the political aspects of the Revolution and this probably accounts for its relatively small role on the Left of the 1820s.

Throughout this study, France was ruled by an ever-changing upper class. Under Napoleon it was the modern upper class, which was imposed by the Emperor as far as the Corps Législatif was concerned and was composed of the Law and Government groups. These same types of men had made the Revolution and the Consulate was set up to insure their rule. Napoleon, however, manipulated this distribution under the Empire by re-introducing the old elites into positions of status. During the One Hundred Days the groups of the Revolution again came forward in the chamber, only to be turned out in the reaction of the Second Restoration which brought back the men of the Old France. The Restoration did not sustain the reaction of August 1815, nor did it return to the revolutionary orientation except briefly in 1817–1819. Instead, the Restoration's deputies were divided between the nobility and the bourgeoisie, with the Proprietor in the strongest position and the men of the Revolution, especially those in Law, submerged. However, progress was occurring and the Revolution had taken place—the government could not overcome these basic facts. By 1830 progress won and the Old France was overthrown; the old social classifications died and the modern ones, even though still fuzzy in outline, began to take their place. The modern upper class took control of the legislature. In France this meant strong landed, legal, and business representation where distinctions between noble and roturier were not critical (see fig. 37).

This view of the entire period, and especially of the role of the Revolution of 1830, is supported in the analysis of the type of department a deputy represented. It was only possible to make this analysis for the period 1815 to 1834, but it clearly shows the correlation between the more advanced and wealthy areas and political opinion in support of the Revolution. Business, as measured by *patentes*, was one part of this correlation, but to

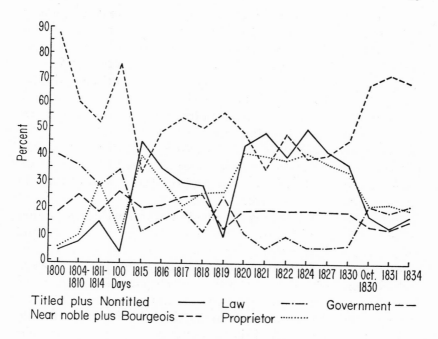

Titled plus Nontitled ——— Law —·—· Government — —
Near noble plus Bourgeois - - - Proprietor ·········

Fig. 37. Deputies: The changing upper class.

focus just on this aspect is to distort the findings. *Patentes* also represented wealth, whereas *Industrial workers* represented change. The cluster of these two variables and *Population size* had significant correlations only with the elections of 1824, 1827, and 1830. The areas that were high on these variables were alienated from the Restoration. The political rhetoric of the day was concerned with the fear that Charles X would reverse the Revolution and its progress. It was progress, which was often a mental phenomenon, that was inhibited by the Restoration, not capitalism or industrialization. That is, freedom as well as social status was being denied to the bourgeoisie and the offices of the state were being blocked to them. The Revolution was in danger of being reversed.

This fear for the progress achieved in the Revolution reached peaks that coincided with other political events. After the chaos of the One Hundred Days, a reaction against the traditions of the Revolution did not seem so bad to the electorate; but by 1817–1819 it did. However, the Left was too radical for the electorate in 1817–1819 and this had unfortunate consequences. The reaction against the revolutionary traditions returned in 1820; the events from 1815 to 1820 seemed to affect all of France, but as the reaction settled in during the early 1820s the country began to divide. The more progressive and wealthy regions began to fear reaction. This became clear in 1827 and 1830. The Revolution of 1830 was forced on France by the government's inability to see the alienation of these areas of France. With the Revolution of 1830, the split between the progressive and wealthy areas and the less endowed areas disappeared for the moment. The Revolution had been saved and the last aspects of the Old Regime could be discarded.

My analysis of the departments, however, revealed a further phenomenon which cannot be ignored: regionalism. Beyond any social-economic-demographic factors of the individual departments, the different regions of France distinguished themselves from each other in terms of which party they supported. This was true under the Restoration, and even though the pattern changed it remained true under the July Monarchy. I could speculate on the causes of the regionalism, yet I could not make any real contribution toward a complete explanation. Regional distribution of parties in France was first discovered during the twentieth century, where it still exists, but others later found it to exist during the July Monarchy.[10] I have pushed it back to 1815 and there are strong indications of its existence back to the Revolution and before. The forces of local traditions are difficult to assess, but there is little doubt that they play a crucial role in politics.

In the final analysis this study has clarified many things we already knew. During the Restoration, the Left's attachment to the Revolution and the Right's attachment to an opposition to the Revolution are exactly what was expected. That the Restoration had many nobles and the July Monarchy had many bourgeois is also not surprising. I hope, however, that these facts are now accurately measured and that they have been put into proper perspective. No longer should historians use data on the deputies which is incomplete and thereby possibly misleading,

---

[10] Patrick and Trevor Higonnet, "Class Corruption and Politics in the French Chamber of Deputies, 1846–1848," *French Historical Studies* 5 (Fall, 1967).

as others have done before.[11] We may now characterize the first third of the nineteenth century by the traditional periods and be clearer on what we mean. There was an evolution toward compromise under Napoleon, which the First Restoration cut short by its failure. The One Hundred Days was a reaction back toward the Revolution, and the Second Restoration was a reaction against the One Hundred Days. The power of each reaction is shown by the turnover in the Chamber and the differences in the type of man elected. A new generation appeared in August 1815 which was to dominate the elections until 1827 with only the short hiatus of the radical Left of 1817–1819. The country, however, could not live with reaction forever, since another generation born during and after the Revolution was coming of age. Its concerns were not the conflicts of the Revolution, but rather that the fundamental results of the Revolution be preserved. Time agreed; the new forces swept to victory in the Revolution of 1830 and ended the mistake that was the Restoration.

A new and different generation appeared under the July Monarchy. This generation would develop its own issues, but these issues would not concern the basic facts of the Revolution as the Restoration had. The July Monarchy was still thrashing out the new society based upon what France actually was—an agricultural and commercial society which had had a revolution from below based upon the Rights of Man. The New France came of age in 1830: whether this was to be an industrial France was not yet the question. That question would have to wait until a later day.

[11] Charléty, *La Restauration*, p. 331.

APPENDIX A: CLASSIFICATION
FOR EACH CATEGORY

Social Class

1. Titled Old Regime nobility: titles 1–4 and 6–7.
2. Nontitled Old Regime nobility as identified by the "de" before the surname. Those with the "de" after the surname and before the man's place of origin were excluded here.
3. Imperial nobility, that is, those who held a title granted by Napoleon: titles 5, 8, and 9.
4. Restoration nobility, that is, those granted titles by Louis XVIII. These men were few in number and were included in the Titled Old Regime nobility.
5. Titled Old Regime nobility who also had a title granted by Napoleon. These men were few in number and were included in the Imperial nobility.
6. Imperial nobility who were also granted a title by Louis XVIII. These men were few in number and were included in the Imperial nobility.
7. Near noble. These included those who added a "de" to their names on their own volition, those whose fathers were described as *ecuyer, rentier,* or *seigneur* on the birth certificate, or those whose father held one of the following positions: *conseiller du roi, trésurier de France,* or *avocat au parlement.*
8. Bourgeois. All of those not included in a previous group.

Titles

1. Prince
2. Duke
3. Marquis

4. Count
5. Count of the Empire
6. Viscount
7. Baron
8. Baron of the Empire
9. Chevalier of the Empire

Occupation

1. Military: Included were army, navy, military administration, and military engineers.
2. Law: Included were *President du parlement, conseiller au parlement, avocat au parlement, avocat, juriconsulte, homme de loi, avoué, notaire, huisser, greffier,* and professor of law.
3. Professions: Included were medical doctors, surgeons, architects, surveyors, engineers, pharmacists, writers, and teachers.
4. Business: Included were *maître de forge, fabricant, industriel, manufacturier, agent de change, negociant, armateur, marchant,* and *banquier.*
5. Government: Included were all paid government positions.
6. Proprietor: Included were *propriétaire, seigneur, ecuyer, agriculteur, cultivateur, fermier,* and all others without an identifiable occupation or source of income.

Honors

1. Order of Saint Louis
2. Chevalier of the Legion of Honor
3. Both 1 and 2
4. Officer of the Legion of Honor
5. Both 1 and 4
6. Commander of the Legion of Honor
7. Both 1 and 6
8. Grand Officer of the Legion of Honor

Taxes Paid

1. Below 1,000 francs: Included were those whose income was below 2,000 francs.
2. 1,000–1,499 francs: Included were those whose income was from 2,000 to 7,000 francs.
3. 1,500–4,999 francs: Included were those whose income was

from 7,000 to 30,000 francs or whose wealth was below 100,000 francs.

4. 5,000 and over: Included were those whose income was over 30,000 francs or whose wealth was over 100,000 francs.

Government Experience

Time Periods

    Old Regime: Prior to July 1789.

    Revolution: 1789–1799.

    Napoleonic: 1800–1814 (with initial breakdown of 1800–1808 and 1809–1814).

    First Restoration: April 1814 to March 1815.

    One Hundred Days: March 1815 to July 1815.

    Second Restoration: August 1815 to September 1816.

    1816–1819:   September 1816 to February 1820.

    1820s: February 1820 to July 1830.

    July Monarchy: August 1830 to December 1834.

Types of Positions Held

    Military: Active duty.

    Magistrature: All positions above Justice of the Peace.

    National Administration: Member of ministries, Financial administration, Administration of Bridges and Roads, Members of Royal or Imperial Household, Council of State, and Prefects.

    Intermediate Administration: Subprefect, Secretary-General of Prefecture, Master of Petitions, Auditors to Council of State, and where label "Departmental Administration" was used. (This occurred during the Revolution.)

    Local Administration: Council-General, Council of Prefecture, Mayor, Vice-Mayor, Justice of Peace, Administration of Water and Forests.

Emigration

    Length: 1790–1814

                1790–1800

                1792–1814

                1792–1800

    Activity: Fought with Army of Princes or in the Vendée. None.

One Hundred Days

  Supporter of Napoleon: Accepted position with the govern-
    ment at any level, made known publicly his support.
  Opposed Napoleon: Resigned office, emigrated, made known
    publicly his opposition.

Party

Right
  1815:   Majority
  1816–1819:   Right, Right-Center, Opposition
  1820–1824:   Right, Right-Center, Supporter of Government,
    Supporter of Villèle, Royalist.
  1827–1830:   Right, Right-Center, Center if not among the
    221, Supporter of Polignac, Resigned August
    1830.
  1831–1834:   Right, Right-Center, Center, Conservative Ma-
    jority, Ministerial, Supporter of Government,
    Supporter of Guizot.
Left
  1815:   Minority, Supporter of King.
  1816–1819:   Left, Opposition.
  1820–1824:   Left, Left-Center, Opposition.
  1827–1830:   Extreme Left, Left, Left-Center, Center, Sup-
    porter of Martignac, Constitutional Royalist,
    Opposition.
  1831–1834:   Extreme Left, Left, Left-Center, Dynastic Op-
    position, Third Party, Supporter of Thiers.
Center
  1816–1819:   Center, Center-Left, Supporter of Government,
    Supporter of Decaze.
Extreme Right
  1824–1830:   Counter-Opposition, Extreme Right, Right and
    among the 221.
  1831–1834:   Legitimist, Supporter of the Bourbons.

  Many men are described as a follower of one of the prominent leaders and in such cases the deputy is classified in the
same party as his leader. Also, many men had more than one
of these labels and I used my judgement to decide which best
represented their dominant position for their final designation.

Regions

1. North: Nord, Pas-de-Calais, Somme.
2. Champagne: Aisne, Aube, Marne.
3. East: Ardennes, Meurthe-et-Moselle, Meuse, Moselle, Bas-Rhin, Haut-Rhin, Vosges.
4. Mountains: Ain, Doubs, Drôme, Isère, Jura, Rhône, Haute-Saône.
5. South: Basses-Alpes, Hautes-Alpes, Aude, Bouches-du-Rhône, Gard, Hérault, Pyrénées-Orientales, Var, Vaucluse.
6. Aquitaine: Ariège, Aveyron, Haute-Garonne, Gers, Lot, Lot-et-Garonne, Hautes-Pyrénées, Tarn, Tarn-et-Garonne.
7. South Coast: Dordogne, Gironde, Landes, Basses-Pyrénées.
8. Central Mountains: Ardèche, Cantal, Corrèze, Creuse, Loire, Haute-Loire, Lozère, Puy-de-Dôme, Haute-Vienne.
9. Lower West: Charente, Charente-Inférieure, Deux-Sèvres, Vendée, Vienne.
10. West: Côtes-du-Nord, Finistère, Ille-et-Vilaine, Loire-Inférieure, Maine-et-Loire, Morbihan, Mayenne, Sarthe.
11. Center: Allier, Cher, Côte-d'Or, Eure-et-Loire, Indre, Indre-et-Loire, Loiret, Loir-et-Cher, Haute-Marne, Nièvre, Saône-et-Loire, Yonne.
12. Channel: Calvados, Eure, Manche, Orne, Seine-Inférieure.
13. Paris Area: Oise, Seine, Seine-et-Marne, Seine-et-Oise.

Corse is omitted from this analysis.

APPENDIX B: DEPARTMENTAL DATA
AND ANALYSIS

TABLE 1
Data for the Social–Economic–Demographic Variables

Department	Population size 1821 (x 1,000)	Population density, 1821 (per km²)	Population of communes 1821 (x 1,000)	Percent population change, 1821–1836	Percent population change of communes 1821–1836[a]	Percent urban	Students (x 10)
Ain	329	56.7	0	5.3	0.0	7.4	54
Aisne	460	62.5	16	14.7	30.9	13.2	102
Allier	280	38.3	14	10.4	9.7	11.5	10
Basses-Alpes	149	21.5	0	6.5	0.0	15.1	52
Hautes-Alpes	121	21.6	0	8.0	0.0	8.0	97
Ardèche	304	55.1	0	16.2	0.0	9.1	38
Ardennes	267	51.0	12	14.9	14.0	14.0	135
Ariège	235	45.9	0	10.9	0.0	10.7	26
Aube	231	38.4	25	10.0	1.9	25.4	123
Aude	253	42.0	26	11.0	54.9	21.7	38
Aveyron	339	38.8	0	9.3	5.0	11.5	22
Bouches-du-Rhône	314	61.4	152	15.5	25.6	71.2	51
Calvados	493	89.1	58	1.9	0.0[b]	21.7	62
Cantal	252	43.9	0	4.0	0.0	8.8	14
Charente	348	58.5	15	5.1	12.7	8.2	42
Charente-Inférieure	409	59.9	29	9.8	3.1	15.3	41
Cher	240	33.3	19	15.6	33.9	15.9	23
Corrèze	273	46.7	0	10.6	0.0	8.9	10
Corse	180	20.6	0	15.3	31.3	13.9	53
Côte-d'Or	358	40.9	32	7.7	9.5	16.1	110
Côtes-du-Nord	552	80.1	0	9.6	14.4	7.0	19
Creuse	249	44.6	0	11.0	0.0	5.6	18
Dordogne	453	49.3	0	7.6	16.3	6.4	14
Doubs	243	46.2	26	13.9	12.6	16.6	132
Drôme	274	41.9	0	11.7	10.2	17.5	77
Eure	416	69.9	0	2.1	3.9	11.7	69
Eure-et-Loire	264	45.0	14	7.8	8.8	13.2	90
Finistère	483	70.9	28	13.2	7.2	13.1	11
Gard	334	57.3	39	9.6	43.3	40.2	64
Haute-Garonne	391	64.9	52	16.3	47.9	22.2	42
Gers	301	48.0	0	3.8	5.1	10.4	32
Gironde	522	53.6	89	6.5	10.7	25.8	27
Hérault	324	52.3	62	10.4	1.9	43.1	50
Ille-et-Vilaine	533	79.2	30	2.6	20.2	14.4	21
Indre	230	33.9	22	11.8	18.6	19.2	21
Indre-et-Loire	282	46.2	22	7.8	21.6	15.1	25
Isère	506	61.0	37	13.5	21.7	11.8	18
Jura	302	60.4	0	4.5	1.9	17.1	110
Landes	256	28.5	0	11.2	0.0	7.1	28
Loir-et-Cher	228	35.8	14	7.3	4.1	14.3	37
Loire	343	72.1	19	20.1	99.9 (117.4)[c]	19.0	61
Haute-Loire	277	55.8	15	6.7	0.5	11.7	8
Loire-Inférieure	434	62.1	68	8.5	10.9	23.1	12
Loiret	291	43.0	40	8.5	0.1	23.4	45
Lot	275	52.7	12	4.3	1.6	10.8	26
Lot-et-Garonne	330	61.6	12	4.9	99.9	15.1	28

Percent literate	Number of voters 1817 (x 10)	Number of voters 1831 (x 10)	Patentes (x 100)	Industrial workers (x 100)	Industrial production (in francs x 1,000)	Agricultural revenue (in francs x 100,000)	Agricultural yield (bushels per hectare)	Agricultural production (in hectares x 100)
43.6	60	110	123	23	16	18	26	45
57.7	142	222	314	217	52	31	36	92
16.5	78	146	91	60	30	13	15	63
50.0	15	48	55	14	3	5	6	32
75.3	11	39	40	7	3	4	6	27
32.9	55	82	96	89	38	13	19	38
69.8	55	123	203	344	177	14	17	46
23.9	35	69	76	51	12	9	15	38
67.1	49	121	189	118	25	15	21	41
38.4	184	196	115	60	21	17	23	89
42.8	144	144	93	64	14	15	15	59
44.4	273	252	184	129	146	19	27	39
65.6	230	419	183	198	69	37	55	58
41.4	85	111	74	21	11	10	15	44
39.0	130	219	121	74	29	19	27	72
42.8	282	246	190	176	24	25	30	88
18.1	96	106	88	23	9	11	13	60
14.3	58	86	68	33	12	9	13	45
53.4	30	30	—	—	—	—	—	—
65.0	140	236	224	45	31	25	25	58
22.9	71	150	107	68	31	20	23	54
25.6	45	74	52	35	15	7	10	42
20.8	139	226	115	47	33	22	21	81
82.5	65	103	93	70	20	13	21	34
47.7	68	113	130	75	62	14	18	60
53.3	257	279	215	232	117	29	40	44
59.1	228	211	145	43	42	22	31	70
17.9	57	145	113	106	12	16	20	65
45.6	68	240	166	256	45	18	26	67
35.0	147	325	182	61	41	23	31	74
39.9	131	180	140	41	25	17	22	71
44.2	217	404	271	83	62	40	32	91
49.8	186	304	162	210	70	20	27	72
42.1	101	183	137	202	40	21	26	65
19.4	62	104	83	48	18	10	12	70
30.0	168	225	151	47	26	15	21	50
39.5	129	229	200	137	38	24	24	67
77.0	63	104	107	15	7	16	27	45
32.0	52	109	79	60	18	7	6	40
31.5	82	145	113	36	16	19	24	68
42.1	92	166	107	507	131	14	25	25
31.3	42	92	57	6	2	11	19	37
33.5	88	201	150	295	162	19	24	83
45.6	166	234	151	58	36	12	17	63
29.2	71	124	75	6	12	12	19	49
33.2	154	254	113	62	29	22	35	62

TABLE 1 (*Cont.*)

Department	Population size 1821 (x 1,000)	Population density, 1821 (per km²)	Population of communes 1821 (x 1,000)	Percent population change, 1821–1836	Percent population change of communes 1821–1836[a]	Percent urban	Students (x 10)
Lozère	134	25.9	0	5.8	0.0	8.9	61
Maine-et-Loire	443	62.1	42	7.8	12.7	15.2	31
Manche	594	99.9 (100.2)[c]	16	0.0	23.3	12.6	75
Marne	308	37.6	43	12.2	20.1	20.7	120
Haute-Marne	233	37.5	0	9.7	0.0	12.2	154
Mayenne	344	66.5	15	5.2	16.9	11.7	37
Meurthe-et-Moselle	380	62.4	40	11.7	9.3	20.0	140
Meuse	291	46.8	11	9.0	0.8	15.2	149
Morbihan	416	61.2	28	8.1	7.7	12.7	9
Moselle	376	70.0	42	13.5	0.7	16.8	123
Nièvre	258	37.9	14	15.3	21.2	13.7	26
Nord	906	99.9 (159.3)[c]	172	13.3	0.0[b]	38.9	87
Oise	376	64.2	13	6.1	2.2	12.0	114
Orne	423	69.4	14	4.9	0.0[b]	10.7	52
Pas-de-Calais	627	94.9	57	6.1	19.9	24.6	123
Puy-de-Dôme	553	69.6	54	6.5	0.0[b]	17.5	18
Basses-Pyrénées	399	52.4	25	11.7	15.5	14.1	70
Hautes-Pyrénées	212	46.8	0	15.1	26.9	13.9	67
Pyrénées-Orientales	143	34.7	13	14.9	40.9	25.6	26
Bas-Rhin	503	99.9 (110.3)[c]	50	11.8	16.5	31.4	143
Haut-Rhin	370	90.1	14	20.8	99.9 (210.7)[c]	27.2	114
Rhône	391	99.9 (140.6)[c]	190	23.1	0.0[b]	43.2	58
Haute-Saône	308	57.7	0	11.4	0.0	9.7	116
Saône-et-Loire	498	58.3	22	8.1	58.6	13.1	45
Sarthe	428	69.1	18	9.0	31.7	12.5	41
Seine	822	99.9 (1731.0)[c]	731	34.6	24.3	92.2	40
Seine-et-Marne	303	52.8	0	7.5	0.0	14.5	84
Seine-et-Oise	424	75.7	27	5.9	6.5	20.2	84
Seine-Inférieure	656	99.9 (108.6)[c]	137	9.9	0.0[b]	26.9	69
Deux-Sèvres	280	46.6	15	8.7	17.4	10.9	46
Somme	509	83.3	61	8.6	6.1	19.3	111
Tarn	314	54.6	25	10.5	16.4	20.1	27
Tarn-et-Garonne	238	64.0	25	1.7	35.4	25.2	26
Var	306	50.2	43	6.0	11.1	47.3	40
Vaucluse	224	63.2	29	9.6	8.1	44.1	50
Vendée	317	47.2	0	7.8	0.0	8.2	34
Vienne	261	37.4	21	10.5	4.1	14.6	26
Haute-Vienne	272	49.2	25	7.6	18.9	17.1	16
Vosges	358	58.8	0	14.9	0.0	11.1	101
Yonne	333	44.8	12	6.7	0.0[b]	14.6	84
Mean	354.2	56.80	35.38	9.88	14.99	18.64	58.4
Standard Deviation	136.7	19.10	83.48	5.08	20.96	13.26	39.7

[a] When a department appeared in this category for the first time I used 9950 as the base population in calculating the percent change.

[b] The actual figure was below 0.0, but negative numbers could not be handled.

Percent literate	Number of voters 1817 (x 10)	Number of voters 1831 (x 10)	Patentes (x 100)	Industrial workers (x 100)	Industrial production (in francs x 1,000)	Agricultural revenue (in francs x 100,000)	Agricultural yield (bushels per hectare)	Agricultural production (in hectares x 100)
37.1	23	62	38	11	2	7	11	32
28.7	144	227	176	101	27	24	29	83
65.5	164	292	153	75	26	32	41	74
71.1	110	194	242	206	76	19	20	65
75.4	48	101	172	73	27	13	17	45
31.3	127	144	91	88	24	15	25	58
68.0	70	159	242	179	28	18	24	51
78.2	55	106	233	76	22	16	22	21
17.4	41	121	102	120	67	16	20	59
60.2	211	150	204	135	26	19	26	44
21.6	64	102	111	62	21	14	17	48
51.1	216	560	423	999 (1069)°	246	50	70	95
63.4	115	248	258	128	48	27	40	81
53.8	117	206	145	157	44	22	29	68
55.0	192	375	255	205	43	36	45	78
24.3	141	236	135	197	41	23	24	77
51.5	32	96	113	120	30	15	17	56
57.4	15	45	75	16	23	8	14	34
34.8	45	84	63	18	6	8	16	52
58.2	57	151	271	108	26	25	42	40
72.6	58	155	174	610	129	18	37	38
59.7	168	366	242	999 (1359)°	328	22	39	34
68.2	52	94	142	84	28	17	32	42
36.2	218	277	177	92	86	30	30	58
36.7	160	226	161	184	55	21	28	46
79.5	999 (12842)°	999 (14865)°	725	89	401	54	99 (216)°	11
61.6	99	290	187	46	29	28	40	85
62.8	96	289	281	84	56	34	51	93
50.5	407	639	383	869	250	47	68	56
47.1	99	141	92	38	12	16	24	45
49.1	189	350	234	171	63	32	45	66
29.7	59	222	125	77	16	17	25	77
28.7	92	185	81	26	21	17	39	40
37.1	59	166	156	41	10	23	27	37
42.1	56	89	108	78	37	12	30	31
32.3	74	137	109	108	43	16	20	49
28.0	108	167	108	28	26	12	15	39
15.0	102	150	77	106	23	9	13	44
67.0	37	83	142	105	25	13	19	45
50.4	93	156	197	14	4	18	21	52
45.24	119.6	195.0	155.2	133.4	50.8	19.2	26.5	55.7
17.52	119.1	137.7	96.7	185.5	67.9	9.5	14.3	18.5

° The figure in the parenthesis is the true figure which had to be reduced to meet the size of the variable. This reduction of a few large figures helps keep such departments from skewing the distribution.

TABLE 2
THE SIGNIFICANT (ABOVE .225) CORRELATIONS OF THE REFINED
SED VARIABLES

	Left	Center	Right
1815	*Students:* .259	—	*Students:* —.259
1816	None	*Students:* .265	*Students:* —.304
1817–1819	None	None	None
1820	None	—	None
1821–1822	*Students:* .341		*Students:* —.338
	Patentes: .277	—	*Patentes:* —.277
1824	*Patentes:* .381		
	Percent population	—	*Patentes:* —.382
	change: .370		*Percent population*
	Industrial		*change:* —.373
	workers: .263		*Industrial*
			workers: —.263
1827	*Patentes:* .463	—	*Patentes:* —.384
	Students: .321		*Students:* —.293
1830	*Patentes:* .402	—	*Patentes:* —.352
	Students: .325		*Students:* —.262
	Industrial		
	workers: .234		
1831	None	—	None
1834	None	—	None

TABLE 3

FACTOR CORRELATIONS

BETWEEN THE CLUSTERS AND THE RESULTS OF THE ELECTIONS

(THE LEFT UNLESS OTHERWISE STATED)

	Cluster 1 (reliability .97)	Cluster 2 (reliability .81)
1815	.032	.193
1816	.025	.079
	.140 Center	.189 Center
1817–1819	.089	.158
	—.004 Center	.044 Center
1820	—.094	—.026
1821–1822	.156	.225
1824	.325	.407
1827	.339	.451
1830	.319	.448
1831	—.117	—.189
1834	.022	.051

Cluster 1: Population size, Population density, Patentes, Voters 1817, Voters 1831, Agricultural revenue, Agricultural yield, and Industrial production.

Cluster 2: Population size, Patentes, Industrial workers, and Election of 1824.

TABLE 4
CORRELATION MATRIX

	Pop. size	Pop. density	Pop. of communes	Pop. change	Pop. change communes	Percent urban	Students
Population size	1.000	.819	.551	.117	.023	.338	.045
Population density	.819	1.000	.445	.115	.143	.385	.165
Population of communes	.551	.445	1.000	.571	.028	.793	—.020
Population change	.117	.115	.571	1.000	.288	.493	.105
Pop. change communes	.023	.143	.028	.288	1.000	.150	—.062
Percent urban	.338	.385	.793	.493	.150	1.000	.066
Students	.045	.165	—.020	.105	—.062	.066	1.000
Percent literate	.115	.211	.227	.168	—.066	.234	.852
Voters, 1817	.607	.468	.869	.347	.065	.621	—.046
Voters, 1831	.777	.643	.811	.252	.061	.620	.015
Patentes	.738	.607	.782	.386	—.019	.616	.359
Industrial workers	.506	.594	.288	.322	.131	.310	.193
Industrial production	.570	.575	.777	.566	.114	.645	.091
Agricultural revenue	.867	.724	.583	.070	.041	.440	.183
Agricultural yield	.768	.792	.703	.204	.101	.577	.219
Agricultural production	.366	.143	—.153	—.310	.001	—.156	—.125
Right 1815	—.053	—.037	—.056	—.214	—.015	—.029	—.259
Left 1815	.054	.038	.051	.211	.015	.026	.259
Right 1816	—.170	—.225	—.014	—.001	—.019	.086	—.304
Center 1816	.143	.215	.026	—.049	.013	—.054	.265
Left 1816	.083	.053	—.016	.107	.015	—.072	.115
Right 1817–1819	—.166	—.018	.011	.048	—.021	.108	—.167
Center 1817–1819	—.041	—.039	.017	—.126	.039	.042	.144
Left 1817–1819	.161	.049	—.023	.075	.020	—.117	—.003
Right 1820	.081	.022	.116	—.154	—.190	.087	—.222
Left 1820	—.081	—.022	—.116	.154	.190	—.087	.222
Right 1821–1822	—.048	—.076	—.162	—.219	—.009	—.120	—.338
Left 1821–1822	.050	.079	.162	.219	.008	.120	.341
Right 1824	—.215	—.223	—.267	—.373	—.225	—.207	—.189
Left 1824	.215	.224	.265	.370	.224	.206	.189
Right 1827	—.137	—.097	—.195	—.059	.005	—.082	—.293
Left 1827	.203	.128	.234	.083	—.092	.137	.321
Right 1830	—.182	—.189	—.113	—.118	—.046	.025	—.262
Left 1830	.214	.217	.143	.159	.073	.018	.325
Right 1831	.133	.137	.022	.134	—.008	—.063	.158
Left 1831	—.114	—.129	—.047	—.165	.021	—.012	—.114
Right 1834	—.041	—.085	.035	.054	—.052	.026	.185
Left 1834	.068	.096	—.059	—.111	.071	—.190	—.139

Percent literate	Voters, 1817	Voters, 1831	Patentes	Ind. workers	Ind. prod.	Agric. revenue	Agric. yield	Agric. Prod.	Right 1815[d]
.115	.607	.777	.738	.506	.570	.867	.768	.366	—.053
.211	.468	.643	.607	.594	.575	.724	.792	.143	—.037
.227	.869	.811	.782	.288	.777	.583	.703	—.153	—.056
.168	.347	.252	.386	.322	.566	.070	.204	—.310	—.214
—.066	.065	.061	—.019	.131	.114	.041	.101	.001	—.015
.234	.621	.620	.616	.310	.645	.440	.577	—.156	—.029
.852	—.046	.015	.359	.193	.091	.183	.219	—.125	—.259
1.000	.188	.214	.458	.202	.278	.300	.374	—.174	—.200
.188	1.000	.885	.781	.230	.687	.718	.761	.035	—.006
.214	.885	1.000	.860	.462	.750	.890	.890	.240	.056
.458	.781	.860	1.000	.451	.731	.844	.849	.139	—.182
.202	.230	.462	.451	1.000	.737	.450	.476	.089	—.010
.278	.687	.750	.731	.737	1.000	.598	.690	—.086	.014
.300	.718	.890	.844	.450	.598	1.000	.911	.418	—.003
.374	.761	.890	.849	.476	.690	.911	1.000	.176	—.020
—.174	.035	.240	.139	.089	—.086	.418	.176	1.000	.169
—.200	—.006	.056	—.182	—.010	.014	—.003	—.020	.169	1.000
.198	.002	—.058	.179	.010	—.017	.002	.018	—.166	—1.000
—.246	—.015	—.022	—.194	—.066	—.030	—.130	—.185	.042	.503
.211	.026	.056	.168	.072	.044	.133	.184	—.043	—.339
.103	—.014	—.061	.083	—.002	—.020	.016	.033	—.004	—.400
—.094	—.090	—.021	—.131	—.017	—.029	—.204	—.125	—.063	.225
.157	.014	.041	—.014	—.065	—.054	.006	.059	—.065	.059
—.069	.055	—.021	.110	.070	.070	.149	.042	.106	—.222
—.147	.131	.183	.005	—.029	.040	.103	.088	.086	.368
.147	—.131	—.183	—.005	.029	—.040	—.103	—.088	—.086	—.368
—.358	—.152	—.106	—.277	—.093	—.151	—.098	—.153	.059	.475
.360	.153	.108	.277	.094	.151	.100	.160	—.058	—.476
—.248	—.248	—.274	—.382	—.263	—.333	—.273	—.304	—.048	.282
.249	.248	.274	.381	.263	.331	.274	.305	.050	—.281
—.322	—.251	—.323	—.384	—.139	—.193	—.315	—.283	—.210	.128
.357	.270	.362	.463	.188	.253	.362	.310	.214	—.043
—.233	—.226	—.238	—.352	—.189	—.220	—.267	—.237	—.169	.087
.304	.260	.281	.402	.234	.245	.309	.278	.198	—.081
.076	.020	.076	.129	.182	.132	.147	.132	.092	.163
—.029	—.025	—.065	—.109	—.171	—.147	—.115	—.105	—.071	—.227
.132	.031	.000	.080	—.012	—.032	.015	.015	—.009	.001
—.074	—.018	.011	—.060	.034	.030	.015	.008	.039	—.061

[d] For 1815, 1820, 1821–1822, and 1824 the figures for the Left are the same as for the Right except for the sign and in a few cases where there is a small, usually 0.001, difference due to rounding errors.

TABLE 4 *(Cont.)*

	Right 1816	Center 1816	Left 1816	Right 1817–19	Center 1817–19	Left 1817–19	Right 1820ᵈ
Population size	—.170	.143	.083	—.166	—.041	.161	.081
Population density	—.225	.215	.053	—.018	—.039	.049	.022
Population of communes	—.014	.026	—.016	.011	.017	—.023	.116
Population change	—.001	—.049	.107	.048	—.126	.075	—.154
Pop. change communes	—.019	.013	.015	—.021	.039	.020	—.190
Percent urban	.086	—.054	—.072	.108	.042	—.117	.087
Students	—.304	.265	.115	—.167	.144	—.003	—.222
Percent literate	—.246	.211	.103	—.094	.157	—.069	—.147
Voters, 1817	—.015	.026	—.014	—.090	.014	.055	.131
Voters, 1831	—.022	.056	—.061	—.021	.041	—.021	.183
Patentes	—.194	.168	.083	—.131	—.014	.110	.005
Industrial workers	—.066	.072	—.002	—.017	—.065	.070	—.029
Industrial production	—.030	.044	—.020	—.029	—.054	.070	.040
Agricultural revenue	—.130	.133	.016	—.204	.006	.149	.103
Agricultural yield	—.185	.184	.033	—.125	.059	.042	.088
Agricultural production	.042	—.043	—.004	—.063	—.065	.106	.086
Right 1815	.503	—.339	—.400	.225	.059	—.222	.368
Left 1815	—.504	.340	.400	—.225	—.059	.223	—.368
Right 1816	1.000	—.890	—.353	.260	—.021	—.178	.261
Center 1816	—.890	1.000	—.114	—.128	.164	—.048	—.118
Left 1816	—.353	—.114	1.000	—.278	—.265	.444	—.325
Right 1817–1819	.260	—.128	—.278	1.000	—.258	—.516	.174
Center 1817–1819	—.021	.164	—.265	—.258	1.000	—.694	.085
Left 1817-1819	—.178	—.048	.444	—.516	—.694	1.000	—.208
Right 1820	.261	—.118	—.325	.174	.085	—.208	1.000
Left 1820	—.261	.118	.325	—.174	—.085	.208	—1.000
Right 1821–1822	.337	—.149	—.398	.275	.156	—.342	.539
Left 1821–1822	—.338	.151	.398	—.275	—.156	.342	—.539
Right 1824	.148	—.133	—.051	.119	—.003	—.086	.127
Left 1824	—.147	.132	.050	—.119	.001	.087	—.127
Right 1827	.088	—.077	—.033	.231	—.175	—.017	.289
Left 1827	—.056	.008	.107	—.263	.138	.073	—.240
Right 1830	.233	—.197	—.103	.421	—.093	—.231	.310
Left 1830	—.244	.217	.086	—.364	.078	.202	—.327
Right 1831	—.025	.074	—.097	.132	—.091	—.018	.111
Left 1831	—.029	—.020	.105	—.117	.138	—.035	—.091
Right 1834	—.149	.172	—.029	—.100	.222	—.124	.105
Left 1834	.024	—.055	.061	—.012	—.212	.198	—.114

Right 1821–22^d	Right 1824^d	Right 1827	Left 1827	Right 1830	Left 1830	Right 1831	Left 1831	Right 1834	Left 1834
−.048	−.215	−.137	.203	−.182	.214	.133	−.114	−.041	.068
−.076	−.223	−.097	.128	−.189	.217	.137	−.129	−.085	.096
−.162	−.267	−.195	.234	−.113	.143	.022	−.047	.035	−.059
−.219	−.373	−.059	.083	−.118	.159	.134	−.165	.054	−.111
−.009	−.225	.005	−.092	−.046	.073	−.008	.021	−.052	−.071
−.120	−.207	−.082	.137	.025	.018	−.063	−.012	.026	−.190
−.338	−.189	−.293	.321	−.262	.325	.158	−.114	.185	−.139
−.358	−.248	−.322	.357	−.233	.304	.076	−.029	.132	−.074
−.152	−.248	−.251	.270	−.226	.260	.020	−.025	.031	−.018
−.106	−.274	−.323	.362	−.238	.281	.076	−.065	.000	.011
−.277	−.382	−.384	.463	−.352	.402	.129	−.109	.080	−.060
−.093	−.263	−.139	.188	−.189	.234	.182	−.171	−.012	.034
−.151	−.333	−.193	.253	−.220	.245	.132	−.147	−.032	.030
−.098	−.273	−.315	.362	−.267	.309	.147	−.115	.015	.015
−.153	−.304	−.283	.310	−.237	.278	.132	−.105	.015	.008
−.059	−.048	−.210	.214	−.169	.198	.092	−.071	−.009	.039
.475	.282	.128	−.043	.087	−.081	.163	−.227	.001	−.061
−.475	−.280	−.127	.042	−.087	.080	−.164	.227	−.003	.063
.337	.148	.088	−.056	.233	−.244	−.025	−.029	−.149	.024
−.149	−.133	−.077	.008	−.197	.217	.074	−.020	.172	−.055
−.398	−.051	−.033	.107	−.103	.086	−.097	.105	−.029	.061
.275	.119	.231	−.263	.421	−.364	.132	−.117	−.100	−.012
.156	−.003	−.175	.138	−.093	.078	−.091	.138	.222	−.212
−.342	−.086	−.017	.073	−.231	.202	−.018	−.035	−.124	.198
.539	.127	.289	−.240	.310	−.327	.111	−.091	.105	−.114
−.539	−.127	−.289	.240	−.310	.327	−.111	.091	−.105	.114
1.000	.193	.455	−.412	.376	−.414	.189	−.182	.036	−.097
−1.000	−.193	−.455	.412	−.378	.415	−.188	.181	−.035	.097
.193	1.000	.329	−.372	.334	−.360	−.131	.120	.080	−.095
−.192	−1.000	−.329	.372	−.334	.360	.130	−.118	−.081	.096
.455	.329	1.000	−.897	.548	−.640	.067	−.113	−.037	−.050
−.412	−.372	−.897	1.000	−.556	.657	−.017	.042	.086	−.012
.376	.334	.548	−.556	1.000	−.931	.006	−.034	−.024	−.033
−.414	−.360	−.640	.657	−.931	1.000	−.072	−.041	.143	−.044
.189	−.131	.067	−.017	.006	.072	1.000	−.957	.518	−.461
−.182	.120	−.113	.042	−.034	−.041	−.957	1.000	−.466	.484
.036	.080	−.037	.086	−.024	.143	.518	−.466	1.000	−.897
−.097	−.095	−.050	−.012	−.033	−.044	−.461	.484	−.897	1.000

APPENDIX C: DATA FOR THE DEPUTIES

*Percent of Deputies for the Corps Législatif and the Chamber of
Representatives of One Hundred Days*

TABLE 5
ELECTIONS BEFORE AUGUST 1815

	Selected 1800	Elimi- nated 1801	Sitting 1803	Elected 1804– 1810	Elected 1811– 1814	Elected 100 Days
Age:						
Under 40	17	14	18	11	1	13
40–49	39	39	38	35	36	32
50–59	32	34	33	34	36	39
60 and over	8	10	9	19	28	17
Birthdate:						
Before 1760	78	79	76	65	50	36
1760–1769	18	17	20	28	46	42
1770 and after	1	1	2	6	5	22
Social class:						
Titled	1	1	3	3	10	2
Nontitled	3	2	4	4	5	2
Imperial	10	8	20	33	33	22
Near noble	19	19	17	23	29	22
Bourgeois	68	70	56	37	23	53
Occupation:						
Law	39	36	30	35	28	34
Government	18	17	21	25	18	26
Proprietor	5	6	7	10	29	11
Business	9	8	10	10	9	11
Military	6	3	11	12	12	11
Professions	8	7	7	6	4	5
Unknown	13	22	13	2	0	1
Honors:						
Legion of Honor	13	7	22	35	32	19
Officer of L.H.	4	4	12	14	26	13

TABLE 5 (*Cont.*)

	Selected 1800	Elimi-nated 1801	Sitting 1803	Elected 1804–1810	Elected 1811–1814	Elected 100 Days
Date first elected:						
1789	13	18	8	4	7	4
1791	9	7	8	5	4	4
1792	16	16	9	3	2	6
1795–1799	54	48	35	9	14	10
1800–1803	8	11	39	3	1	1
1804–1810	—	—	—	74	2	2
1811–1814	—	—	—	—	70	2
May 1815	—	—	—	—	—	70
Experience in government:						
Old Regime	17	19	22	30	30	13
Revolution	72	71	65	58	47	45
Emigration	0	0	0	3	10	3
Napoleonic	27	23	55	86	77	52
100 Days	—	—	—	—	—	58
Total number of deputies:	278	141	252	225	109	628

Percent of Deputies for the Chamber of Deputies

TABLE 6
Elections of August 1815 and 1816

	August 1815	Eliminated 1816	1816
Age:			
Under 40	14	20	—
40–49	38	30	41
50–59	36	33	41
60 and over	13	17	18
Birthdate:			
Before 1760	26	—	26
1760–1769	41	—	51
1770 and after	33	—	23
Social class:			
Titled	36	42	25
Nontitled	9	9	9
Imperial	12	9	18
Near noble	28	26	27
Bourgeois	15	14	21
Occupation:			
Law	12	11	16
Government	20	21	21
Proprietor	39	37	30
Business	10	5	18
Military	16	24	13
Professions	3	3	3
Taxes paid:			
1,500 and over	64	51	63
Honors:			
Order of St. Louis	31	34	24
Legion of Honor	29	27	31
Officer of L. H.	14	13	17
Total with one	60	63	58
Date first elected:			
1789–1794	7	7	7
1795–1799	4	2	5
1800–1814	6	4	8
May 1815	2	2	6
August 1815	80	84	56
1816	—	—	18

TABLE 6 (*Cont.*)

	August 1815	Eliminated 1816	1816
Experience in government:			
Old Regime	23	24	22
Revolution	20	15	25
Emigration	21	21	20
Napoleonic	46	42	52
100 Days, support	6	5	8
100 Days, opposition	23	20	23
Second Restoration	60	62	58
1816–1819	—	—	61
Party:			
Left:	22	13	10
Center	—	—	44
Right	78	85	44
Total number of deputies:	400	224	240

TABLE 7

ELECTIONS OF AUGUST 1815 AND 1816, BY PARTY

	1815		1816		
	Left	Right	Left	Center	Right
Age:					
Under 40	15	13	—	—	—
40–49	34	39	38	36	46
50–59	39	35	43	44	38
60 and over	14	12	19	20	16
Social class:					
Titled	16	42	10	17	38
Nontitled	3	10	0	5	15
Imperial	33	7	29	24	9
Near noble	24	29	24	25	29
Bourgeois	25	12	38	29	9
Occupation:					
Law	19	10	38	19	9
Government	34	16	14	29	14
Proprietor	15	41	5	20	46
Business	21	8	33	17	15
Military	8	22	0	12	15
Professions	3	2	5	1	1
Taxes paid:					
1500 and over	60	57	62	51	67
Honors:					
Order of St. Louis	16	38	5	17	31
Legion of Honor	34	31	38	32	29
Officer of L. H.	27	10	24	24	7
Total with one	66	59	67	59	53
Date first elected:					
1789–1794	10	6	10	8	4
1795–1799	6	3	14	3	5
1800–1814	14	4	19	11	4
May 1815	14	0	24	8	0
August 1815	57	88	24	45	73
1816	—	—	10	23	14
Experience in government:					
Old Regime	18	29	14	18	26
Revolution	34	20	43	29	17
Emigration	7	24	5	11	32
Napoleonic	74	38	76	68	16
100 Days, support	18	2	29	10	1
100 Days, opposition	25	22	10	25	24
Second Restoration	61	60	33	66	54
1816–1819	—	—	43	71	55

TABLE 7 (*Cont.*)

	1815		1816		
	Left	Right	Left	Center	Right
Region:					
North	15	85	7	64	29
Champagne	54	46	11	55	33
East	55	45	19	81	0
Center	16	84	11	35	54
Mountains	13	87	18	35	47
South	18	82	0	21	79
Central Mts.	20	80	5	35	60
Aquitaine	9	91	4	37	58
South Coast	19	81	0	43	57
Lower West	32	68	14	43	43
West	21	79	10	45	45
Channel	14	86	0	60	40
Paris Area	25	75	13	69	19
National Average	22	78	10	47	44
Votes cast/					
Voters registered:					
Under 50%	7	2	0	0	1
Over 75%	27	23	24	32	32
Over 90%	0	1	0	0	1
Votes received/					
Voters registered:					
Over 50%	22	16	14	17	16
Votes received/					
Votes cast:					
Under 56%	39	32	52	33	38
Over 75%	13	11	29	16	8
Over 90%	6	1	5	5	3
Total number of deputies: *	89	308	21	134	106

* I included by-elections when analyzing the elections by party in order to measure the entire period in this phase of the analysis. I followed this practice in each election until 1827, when the number of by-elections became numerous and the conditions in which they were held differed from those of the general election.

TABLE 8
Elections of 1817–1819

	1817	1818	1819	1817–1819 Left	Center	Right
Age:						
Under 40	—	—	—	—	—	—
40–49	37	37	32	41	27	37
50–59	46	46	41	41	56	29
60 and over	18	18	27	18	17	33
Birthdate:						
Before 1760	22	19	27	—	—	—
1760–1769	48	49	41	—	—	—
1770 and after	30	32	32	—	—	—
Social class:						
Titled	18	23	5	8	17	42
Nontitled	10	4	5	2	6	25
Imperial	19	25	32	29	29	0
Near noble	33	25	29	29	27	33
Bourgeois	21	25	29	32	21	0
Occupation:						
Law	19	12	25	23	17	4
Government	24	26	13	13	32	17
Proprietor	21	26	27	23	11	46
Business	24	23	18	23	23	13
Military	11	9	14	10	12	21
Professions	2	4	4	7	4	0
Taxes paid:						
1,500 and over	54	54	45	47	52	67
Honors:						
Order of St. Louis	22	12	20	12	20	42
Legion of Honor	24	35	22	21	35	21
Officer of L. H.	27	23	32	24	35	17
Total with one	59	62	55	50	70	58
Date first elected:						
1789–1794	5	12	9	9	12	4
1795–1799	8	11	5	10	3	12
1800–1814	5	12	11	8	12	0
May 1815	13	16	18	26	6	0
August 1815	25	16	13	6	24	46
1816	5	2	5	1	8	13
1817–1819	35	26	39	39	33	25
Experience in government:						
Old Regime	14	28	13	18	24	21
Revolution	33	32	50	49	33	8
Emigration	16	12	4	6	14	30
Napoleonic	60	60	62	60	78	33
100 Days, support	14	26	39	39	12	0
100 Days, opposition	16	5	9	3	17	13
Second Restoration	41	42	30	22	59	42
1816–1819	67	49	50	41	74	54

TABLE 8 (*Cont.*)

	1817	1818	1819	1817–1819 Left	Center	Right
Party:						
Left	29	53	70	50		
Center	48	42	21		37	
Right	24	5	9			13
Region:						
North				33	67	0
Champagne				100	0	0
East				62	39	0
Center				32	58	11
Mountain				72	11	17
South				8	50	42
Central Mts.				40	30	30
Aquitaine				9	45	45
South Coast				10	80	10
Lower West				82	18	0
West				79	12	8
Channel				46	50	5
Paris Area				27	60	13
National Average				50	37	13
Votes cast/Voters registered:						
Under 50%				11	15	9
Over 75%				32	24	39
Over 90%				0	0	0
Votes received/Voters registered:						
Over 50%				17	17	9
Votes received/Votes cast:						
Under 56%				29	32	58
Over 75%				8	14	4
Over 90%				0	2	0
Total number of deputies: *	63	57	56	90	66	24

*See note to table 7.

TABLE 9
Elections of 1820–1824

	1820	1821	1822	1824
Age:				
Under 50	37	35	32	33
50–59	45	45	43	43
60 and over	18	20	26	24
Birthdate:				
Before 1760	15	12	16	9
1760–1769	44	41	44	37
1770 and after	40	47	40	54
Social class:				
Titled	35	37	29	39
Nontitled	9	11	12	12
Imperial	9	18	11	9
Near noble	25	20	30	25
Bourgeois	23	15	18	16
Occupation:				
Law	11	6	10	7
Government	19	20	20	20
Proprietor	42	41	40	43
Business	13	12	16	11
Military	12	17	12	15
Professions	4	6	3	3
Taxes paid:				
1,500 and over	65	72	64	64
Honors:				
Order of St. Louis	27	33	26	33
Legion of Honor	41	40	36	45
Officer of L. H.	10	17	10	14
Total with one	65	67	60	71
Date first elected:				
1789–1794	4	2	3	1
1795–1799	3	3	4	3
1800–1814	4	2	2	2
May 1815	2	8	6	1
August 1815	32	33	20	25
1816	5	4	4	2
1817–1819	1	1	8	3
1820	50	17	17	18
1821–1822	—	28	33	14
1824	—	—	—	30
Experience in government:				
Old Regime	17	17	16	16
Revolution	15	17	17	13
Emigration	22	23	23	24
Napoleonic	44	45	37	35
100 Days, support	6	8	10	4
100 Days, opposition	19	27	11	19
Second Restoration	46	52	36	48
1816–1819	46	56	41	49
1820s	66	70	63	81

TABLE 9 (*Cont.*)

	1820	1821	1822	1824
Party:				
Left	17	21	23	8
Right	83	79	77	85
Extreme Right	—	—	—	7
Total number of deputies:	222	91	174	429

TABLE 10
ELECTIONS OF 1820–1824, BY PARTY

	1820		1821–1822		1824		
	Left	Right	Left	Right	Left	Right	Extreme Right
Age:							
Under 50	31	40	38	32	27	33	39
50–59	46	45	41	45	53	42	48
60 and over	23	17	21	26	21	25	12
Social class:							
Titled	10	42	15	36	21	39	51
Nontitled	3	11	0	15	3	12	18
Imperial	15	8	35	9	27	8	9
Near noble	15	27	20	27	18	25	18
Bourgeois	56	16	30	13	32	16	3
Occupation:							
Law	13	10	12	8	9	8	6
Government	15	20	18	19	9	22	9
Proprietor	37	41	24	49	23	43	69
Business	21	11	27	10	32	10	3
Military	13	12	17	14	27	15	12
Professions	3	2	0	1	0	2	0
Taxes paid:							
1,500 and over	46	64	70	65	59	63	76
Honors:							
Order of St. Louis	5	33	17	32	24	38	54
Legion of Honor	26	45	24	42	32	51	48
Officer of L. H.	13	10	27	8	24	13	18
Total with one	39	72	55	65	62	77	84
Date first elected:							
1789–1799	13	5	8	6	21	4	0
1800–1814	3	3	2	2	3	2	3
May 1815	13	0	23	1	21	1	0
August 1815	0	38	8	28	0	26	21
1816	8	3	3	4	0	3	0
1817–1819	8	4	14	3	21	2	0
1820	49	49	21	27	9	16	12
1821–1822	—	—	40	38	6	14	12
1824	—	—	—	—	18	29	42
Experience in government:							
Old Regime	15	19	14	17	15	16	21
Revolution	41	12	41	12	35	12	6
Emigration	3	27	14	26	6	23	42
Napoleonic	44	39	65	33	47	36	24
100 Days, support	31	1	30	2	32	2	0
100 Days, opposition	0	23	9	18	6	18	24
Second Restoration	28	50	24	46	30	48	45
1820s	41	79	32	75	44	82	75

TABLE 10 (*Cont.*)

	1820		1821–1822		1824		
	Left	Right	Left	Right	Left	Right	Extreme Right
Region:							
North	0	100	14	86	0	92	8
Champagne	43	57	33	67	38	63	0
East	62	38	39	61	8	89	3
Center	16	84	28	72	5	89	5
Mountains	0	100	26	74	7	83	10
South	11	89	5	95	0	100	0
Central Mts.	6	94	12	88	12	88	0
Aquitaine	16	84	4	96	0	90	10
South Coast	0	100	0	100	8	88	4
Lower West	36	64	44	56	0	85	15
West	19	81	11	89	4	86	10
Channel	9	91	5	95	7	83	10
Paris Area	0	100	55	45	19	75	6
National Avg.	17	83	23	77	6	87	7
Votes cast/							
Voters registered:							
Under 50%	3	1	0	2	0	0	0
Over 75%	90	92	58	58	88	72	70
Over 90%	26	27	20	8	49	15	6
Votes received/							
Voters registered:							
Over 50%	34	63	42	49	39	70	52
Votes received/							
Votes cast:							
Under 56%	41	19	32	20	44	17	24
Over 75%	5	10	2	26	17	36	36
Over 90%	3	3	0	12	6	16	9
Presidents of Electoral							
College:							
Yes	0	21	3	34	9	59	18
Total number of							
deputies: *	39	187	66	218	34	383	33

*See note to table 7.

TABLE 11
ELECTIONS OF 1827 AND 1830

	Total 1827	Eliminated 1827	Total 1830
Age:			
Under 50	36	16	31
50–59	36	41	42
60 and over	28	43	27
Birthdate:			
Before 1760	7	11	5
1760–1769	27	43	18
1770–1779	40	35	42
1780 and after	27	11	34
Social class:			
Titled	32	39	28
Nontitled	12	11	10
Imperial	13	10	15
Near noble	22	26	22
Bourgeois	21	14	25
Occupation:			
Law	7	7	8
Government	20	20	20
Proprietor	38	43	35
Business	17	10	19
Military	12	18	14
Professions	6	2	5
Taxes paid:			
1,500 and over	60	64	62
Honors:			
Order of St. Louis	25	34	20
Legion of Honor	58	39	47
Officer of L. H.	16	14	18
Total with one	80	68	69
Date first elected:			
1789–1799	7	5	5
1800–1814	2	2	3
May 1815	8	2	7
August 1815	13	26	8
1816	1	2	1
1817–1819	6	2	5
1820	8	18	6
1821–1822	7	14	6
1824	12	31	7
1827	35	—	31
1830	—	—	19

TABLE 11 (*Cont.*)

	Total 1827	Eliminated 1827	Total 1830
Experience in government:			
Old Regime	10	18	8
Revolution	14	14	14
Emigration	14	27	9
Napoleonic	41	35	44
100 Days, support	14	4	15
100 Days, opposition	13	19	11
Second Restoration	36	49	31
1820s	63	77	61
Party:			
Left	44	4	59
Right	49	93	30
Extreme Right	5	3	6
Unknown	2	—	5
Total number of deputies:	429	259	431

TABLE 12
ELECTIONS OF 1827 AND 1830, BY PARTY

	1827			1830		
	Left	Right	Extreme Right	Left	Right	Extreme Right
Age:						
Under 50	31	40	41	29	35	33
50–59	36	34	48	40	42	54
60 and over	32	22	11	31	23	13
Social class:						
Titled	17	44	30	18	40	50
Nontitled	5	17	15	6	16	21
Imperial	22	9	0	14	12	13
Near noble	22	18	33	26	18	17
Bourgeois	35	12	22	36	14	0
Occupation:						
Law	10	5	7	11	4	4
Government	18	22	11	16	26	17
Proprietor	20	51	56	31	45	58
Business	28	6	26	27	7	4
Military	12	15	0	13	15	17
Professions	2	1	0	2	1	0
Taxes paid:						
1,500 and over	59	63	63	61	63	67
Honors:						
Order of St. Louis	14	34	22	14	30	29
Legion of Honor	76	62	56	43	49	58
Officer of L. H.	22	15	15	19	20	13
Total with one	69	86	82	64	79	75
Date first elected:						
1789–1799	11	1	0	6	2	5
1800–1814	3	1	0	3	1	0
May 1815	14	1	0	11	1	0
August 1815	5	20	7	3	16	14
1816	1	2	4	1	4	0
1817–1819	9	2	0	8	1	0
1820	4	10	15	3	9	9
1821–1822	3	9	11	6	9	5
1824	2	18	30	3	12	14
1827	46	34	33	36	28	32
1830	—	—	—	20	15	23
Experience in government:						
Old Regime	10	13	4	8	11	8
Revolution	21	8	0	18	10	4
Emigration	8	18	15	5	14	17
Napoleonic	53	35	15	50	37	25
100 Days, support	24	2	0	20	5	4
100 Days, opposition	9	16	19	6	21	21
Second Restoration	24	46	30	23	47	38
1820s	39	88	78	49	88	67

TABLE 12 (*Cont.*)

	1827			1830		
	Left	Right	Extreme Right	Left	Right	Extreme Right
Region:						
North	31	58	12	52	44	4
Champagne	79	21	0	86	14	0
East	53	38	9	88	12	0
Center	57	36	8	67	24	8
Mountains	54	46	0	64	36	0
South	30	58	10	33	63	3
Central Mts.	24	73	3	45	52	3
Aquitaine	9	84	7	25	57	17
South Coast	52	43	4	73	27	0
Lower West	42	42	17	65	26	9
West	20	74	6	33	56	10
Channel	69	25	6	84	13	3
Paris Area	93	7	0	100	0	0
National Average	44	49	6	60	34	5
Votes cast/						
Voters registered:						
Under 50%	0	2	0	0	0	0
Over 75%	95	70	84	96	92	81
Over 90%	18	8	8	40	36	36
Votes received/						
Voters registered:						
Over 50%	55	34	49	73	62	54
Votes received/						
Votes Cast:						
Under 56%	26	39	33	28	33	27
Over 75%	11	10	30	13	11	14
Over 90%	2	4	15	0	5	14
Presidents of Electoral						
College:						
Yes	2	38	22	1	30	29
Total number						
of deputies:	189	210	27	245	140	22

TABLE 13
Deputies Eliminated in 1827, by Party

	Left	Right
Age:		
Under 50	0	17
50–59	60	40
60 and over	40	43
Social class:		
Titled	10	39
Nontitled	0	11
Imperial	50	9
Near noble	10	27
Bourgeois	30	13
Occupation:		
Law	0	8
Government	10	21
Proprietor	20	43
Business	20	10
Military	50	17
Professions	0	2
Experience in government:		
Revolution	60	12
Emigration	0	27
Napoleonic	80	33
100 Days, support	50	2
100 Days, opposition	0	20
Second Restoration	50	49
1820s	60	78
Total number of deputies:	10	241

TABLE 14
ELECTIONS OF 1820–1830, BY TYPE OF CONSTITUENCY

	1820		1821–1822		1824		1827		1830	
	Dept.	Dist.	Dept.	Dist.	Dept.	Dist.	Dept.	Dist.	Dept.	Dist.
Age:										
Under 50	40	26	40	28	37	32	36	36	29	31
50–59	42	55	39	46	43	42	38	35	44	42
60 and over	17	20	21	26	20	26	26	29	27	27
Social class:										
Titled	43	10	42	25	53	30	42	26	38	22
Nontitled	9	8	14	10	12	12	13	11	11	10
Imperial	7	14	12	14	6	11	7	18	13	17
Near noble	26	22	19	32	21	27	22	22	24	20
Bourgeois	15	47	12	20	9	20	16	25	14	32
Occupation:										
Law	10	14	8	10	7	6	5	8	7	8
Government	18	16	16	22	15	23	19	21	19	21
Proprietor	47	25	50	34	52	38	48	31	45	28
Business	11	20	6	20	6	15	15	19	12	23
Military	11	14	18	11	18	14	11	13	14	14
Professions	4	11	2	3	2	4	2	8	3	6
Honors:										
Order of St. Louis	30	18	39	27	40	30	31	22	24	18
Legion of Honor	42	40	36	39	42	47	65	54	51	44
Officer of L. H.	8	14	14	11	15	14	14	17	19	17
Taxes paid:										
Less than 1500	28	61	28	38	29	39	29	45	36	38
1,500–4,999	58	26	59	49	56	48	62	48	55	54
5,000 and over	13	18	13	13	13	12	7	7	7	8
Date first elected:										
1789–1799	5	12	5	8	2	7	4	8	4	5
1800–1814	2	10	2	2	1	2	1	2	3	2
May 1815	1	8	3	9	0	2	1	11	2	10
August 1815	35	22	24	24	25	25	13	14	8	9
1816	2	11	3	5	1	3	2	1	1	1
1817–1819	0	4	4	8	1	4	2	9	1	9
1820	55	33	27	7	23	15	12	6	8	5
1821–1822	—	—	32	30	13	15	9	6	7	6
1824	—	—	—	—	33	27	15	10	10	6
1827	—	—	—	—	—	—	40	32	28	32
1830	—	—	—	—	—	—	—	—	28	13

TABLE 14 (*Cont.*)

	1820		1821–1822		1824		1827		1830	
	Dept.	Dist.	Dept.	Dist.	Dept.	Dist.	Dept.	Dist.	Dept.	Dist.
Experience in government:										
Old Regime	17	45	22	20	21	18	10	18	10	11
Revolution	11	29	12	20	8	20	9	16	14	15
Emigration	27	6	28	12	30	19	17	11	13	7
Napoleonic	39	82	32	46	29	40	33	47	38	47
100 Days, support	3	18	2	15	1	7	5	19	8	20
100 Days, opposition	20	18	23	14	22	17	13	14	16	9
Second Restoration	49	37	41	43	49	47	37	35	36	28
1820s	74	57	72	61	80	81	76	57	74	57
Party:										
Left	8	43	9	31	3	8	41	47	45	64
Right	92	57	91	69	84	89	51	48	48	24
Extreme Right	—	—	—	—	13	4	8	5	8	4
Total number of deputies:	171	51	107	158	172	257	166	263	168	263

TABLE 15
ELECTIONS OF 1827 AND 1830, DEPARTMENTAL DEPUTIES ONLY

	1827		1830	
	Left	Right	Left	Right
Social class:				
Titled	20	51	24	44
Nontitled	12	13	8	14
Imperial	14	7	16	11
Near noble	24	19	27	25
Bourgeois	30	11	25	6
Occupation:				
Law	8	7	8	5
Government	22	19	18	22
Proprietor	26	52	38	52
Business	36	5	24	4
Military	6	17	10	17
Professions	2	1	3	1
Experience in government:				
Old Regime	6	12	8	11
Revolution	18	7	18	13
Emigration	6	20	5	19
Napoleonic	44	33	44	37
100 Days, support	18	2	14	4
100 Days, opposition	10	15	3	23
Second Restoration	32	43	27	48
1820s	58	86	60	90
Total number of deputies:	50	121	63	79

TABLE 16
Elections of the July Monarchy

	Excluded 1830	October 1830	Total 1831	Eliminated 1831	Began 1831	Total 1834
Age:						
Under 40	—	29	18	6	34	22
40–49	39	33	31	23	34	35
50–59	44	28	29	39	23	28
60 and over	16	9	21	32	11	15
Birthdate:						
Before 1760	—	—	2	—	—	1
1760–1769	—	—	13	—	—	7
1770–1779	—	—	28	—	—	19
1780–1789	—	—	34	—	—	35
1790 and after	—	—	23	—	—	38
Social class:						
Titled	43	13	11	26	4	13
Nontitled	18	6	3	12	3	6
Imperial	10	12	13	15	5	13
Near noble	16	24	24	21	24	24
Bourgeois	12	44	49	27	64	45
Occupation:						
Law	3	23	21	11	27	23
Government	23	15	13	22	13	18
Proprietor	47	23	24	33	20	22
Business	7	15	20	17	19	17
Military	16	19	14	14	9	14
Professions	1	4	8	3	12	7
Taxes paid:						
1,500 and over	66	41	40	60	22	39
Honors:						
Order of St. Louis	27	7	8	19	2	7
Legion of Honor	49	18	24	43	12	23
Officer of L. H.	18	16	14	16	8	13
Total with one	77	34	39	63	20	36
Date first elected:						
1789–1799	1	1	3	5	—	1
1800–1814	3	1	2	2	—	2
May 1815	0	5	8	5	—	5
August 1815	11	1	1	10	—	1
1816	2	1	1	2	—	1
1817–1819	0	1	3	5	—	1
1820	8	0	2	5	—	1
1821–1822	6	0	1	5	—	1
1824	12	1	1	9	—	1
1827	34	7	19	20	—	11
1830	21	2	6	18	—	6
October 1830	—	79	12	14	—	10
1831	—	—	41	—	100	27
1834	—	—	—	—	—	27

TABLE 16 (*Cont.*)

	Excluded 1830	October 1830	Total 1831	Eliminated 1831	Began 1831	Total 1834
Experience in government:						
Old Regime	11	1	5	8	1	2
Revolution	6	17	13	16	5	10
Emigration	15	4	3	9	1	2
Napoleonic	36	40	37	41	22	36
100 Days, support	5	20	22	11	16	17
100 Days, opposition	20	7	4	12	2	6
Second Restoration	47	14	14	28	6	14
1820s	90	18	28	54	13	28
July Monarchy	—	64	64	22	65	70
Party:						
Left	0	90	38	58	46	33
Right	100[a]	4	61	23	53	63
Legitimists	—	—	2	10	2	4
Unknown	—	6	—	9	—	—
Total number of deputies:	99	99	458	196	191	457

[a]For this group the designation is on the basis of the Restoration. Sixty-three percent were Right, 23 percent were in the Counter-Opposition, and 13 percent were identified as only having resigned.

TABLE 17

Elections of 1831 and 1834, by Party

	1831			1834		
	Left	Right	Leg.	Left	Right	Leg.
Age:						
Under 40	28	18	10	31	18	23
40–49	30	33	40	31	35	45
50–59	26	31	20	24	30	23
60 and over	16	18	30	13	17	9
Social class:						
Titled	11	11	40	8	14	36
Nontitled	3	3	10	6	5	14
Imperial	10	14	10	8	15	0
Near noble	23	22	40	22	24	32
Bourgeois	53	50	0	56	43	18
Occupation:						
Law	28	18	30	26	21	46
Government	11	14	20	17	19	14
Proprietor	20	21	30	21	17	27
Business	12	24	0	16	18	0
Military	14	16	20	9	16	9
Professions	14	8	0	10	9	5
Taxes paid:						
1500 and over	33	42	30	31	42	27
Honors:						
Order of St. Louis	4	9	10	3	8	9
Legion of Honor	16	27	50	20	24	18
Officer of L. H.	11	16	10	8	15	9
Total with one	29	43	60	28	39	27
Date first elected:						
1789–1799	4	2	0	1	1	0
1800–1814	1	2	0	1	2	0
May 1815	7	7	0	3	6	0
August 1815	1	2	0	1	1	9
1827	12	17	20	7	12	5
1830	3	7	10	2	7	5
October 1830	10	13	20	11	11	0
1831	54	45	40	33	30	18
1834	—	—	—	35	26	46
Experience in government:						
Old Regime	5	2	10	1	2	5
Revolution	9	14	10	5	13	0
Emigration	4	1	20	1	2	14
Napoleonic	34	35	20	28	37	18
100 Days, support	19	18	10	12	18	0
100 Days, opposition	4	3	30	4	5	32
Second Restoration	13	13	30	9	14	18
1820s	19	30	60	22	31	36
July Monarchy	62	70	30	67	74	23

TABLE 17 (*Cont.*)

| | 1831 | | | 1834 | | |
	Left	Right	Leg.	Left	Right	Leg.
Region:						
North	10	90	0	23	70	7
Champagne	24	76	0	33	67	0
East	34	67	0	22	75	3
Center	39	57	4	31	65	4
Mountains	41	59	0	30	67	3
South	58	36	6	27	54	19
Central Mts.	34	63	3	23	74	3
Aquitaine	36	64	0	38	52	10
South Coast	38	62	0	13	87	0
Lower West	61	35	4	54	46	0
West	29	69	2	45	53	2
Channel	43	58	0	46	54	0
Paris Area	39	61	0	30	70	0
National Average	38	61	2	33	63	4
Votes cast/Voters registered:						
Under 50%	2	4	0	2	1	0
Over 75%	64	54	57	45	63	69
Over 90%	6	3	0	3	3	0
Votes received/						
Voters registered:						
Over 50%	51	43	14	31	31	21
Votes received/Votes cast:						
Under 56%	23	24	43	28	34	58
Over 75%	22	30	14	13	15	0
Over 90%	7	12	0	4	5	0
Total number of deputies:	170	273	7	146	286	18

BIBLIOGRAPHY

Documents

Almanach royal et national de France.
Annuaire statistique de la France, 1966 Résumé rétrospectif.
Archives parlementaires de 1787 à 1860, séries 2.
Bulletin des lois.
Statistique de la France: Industrie, vols. 1–4. Paris, 1852.
Statistique de l'enseignement primaire, vol. 2. Paris, 1880.
Archives nationales (unpublished)
 Procès-verbaux des assemblées nationales:
  Séries C1164–C1323
  Séries CC28–CC49
 Administration générale: Elections
  Séries FicII
 Administration générale: Esprit public et élections
  Séries FicIII

Newspapers

Le Moniteur

Dictionaries

Biographie des députés de la Chambre Septennale de 1824 à 1830. Paris: Chez J.-G. Dentu, 1826.
Biographie pittoresque des députés de France, session de 1819 à 1820. Bruxelles: Chez J. Munbach, 1820.
Biographie speciale des pairs et des députés du royaume, sessions de 1818–1819. Paris: Beaucé, 1819.
Braun, J.-B.-M. *Nouvelle biographie des députés ou statistique de la Chambre de 1814 à 1829.* Paris: Libraire Béchet ainé, 1830.

Brissot-Thivars. *Le guide électoral ou biographie législative de tous les députés depuis 1814 jusques et y compris 1818 à 1819.* Paris: Libraire constitutionnelle, 1819.

Campardon, Emile. *Liste des membres de la noblesse impériale.* Paris: Société de l'histoire de la révolution française, 1889.

Chalet, Bénard-Vallée. *Biographie politique des députés: session de 1831.* Paris: Pagnerre éditeur, 1831.

Dourille, J. *Biographie des députés de la nouvelle chambre septennale: sessions de 1829.* Paris: Chez des Marchands de Nouveautés, 1829.

Gallois, L. *Biographie de tous les ministres.* Paris: Chez tous les Marchands de Nouveautés, 1825.

Lamothe-Langon. *Biographie des préfets des 87 départements de la France.* Paris: Chez des Marchands de Nouveautés, 1826.

Massey de Tyronne, Pierre-François-Marie and Dentu. *Biographie des députés de la Chambre septennale de 1824 à 1830.* Paris: Chez J.-G. Dentu, 1826.

Petit almanach législatif ou la vérité en riant sur nos députés, seconde édition. Paris: Libraire universelle de P. Mongie, 1820.

P. P. *Biographie des députés composant la représentation nationale pendant les sessions de 1820 à 1822.* Paris: Chez Plancher, 1822.

Robert, Adolphe, and Gaston Cougny. *Dictionnaire des parlementaires français.* 5 vols. Paris: Bourolton, 1889–1891.

Tableau des membres composant la Chambre des Députés. Paris: Chez Marchands de Nouveautés, 1822.

Primary Works

Chaptal, Le Comte. *De l'industrie française.* Paris: Chez Antoine-Augustine Renovard, 1819.

Costaz, Cl.-Anthelme. *Essai sur l'administration de l'agriculture, du commerce, des manufactures, et des subsistances.* Paris: Huzard, 1818.

Dupin, Le Baron Charles. *Forces productives et commerciales de la France.* 2 vols. Bruxelles: Jobard Frères, 1828.

Fazy, J.-J. *De la gérontocratie ou abus de la sagesse des vieillards dans le gouvernement de la France.* Paris: Delaforest, 1828.

Montcalm, Marquise de. *Mon journal, 1815–1818, pendant le premier ministère de mon frère.* Paris: Bernard Grasset, 1936.

Moreau de Jonnès. M.A. *Statistique de l'agriculture de la France.* Paris: Libraire de Guillaumin et Cie, 1848.

————. *Statistique de l'industrie de la France.* Paris: Libraire de Guillaumin et Cie, 1856.

Secondary Works

Agulhon, Maurice. *La République au village (Les population du Var de la Révolution à la Seconde République).* Paris: Libraire Plon, 1970.

————. *La Vie sociale en Provence intérieure au lendemain de la Révolution.* Paris: Société des Etudes Robespierristes, 1970.

Artz, Frederick B. *France under the Bourbon Restoration, 1814–1830.* New York: Russell and Russell, 1931.

Bastid, Paul. *Les institutions politiques de la monarchie parlementaire française, 1814–1848.* Paris: Editions du Receuil Sirey, 1954.

Beau de Loménie, Emmanuel. *Les résponsabilités des dynasties bourgeoises. De Bonaparte à Mac-Mahon,* vol. 1. Paris: Editions Denoil, 1943.

Bertier de Sauvigny, Guillaume de. *The Bourbon Restoration.* Philadelphia: University of Pennsylvania Press, 1966.

Block, Maurice. *Statistique de la France.* Paris: Guillaumin et Cie, 1875.

Cameron, Rondo E. *France and the Economic Development of Europe, 1800–1914.* Princeton: Princeton University Press, 1961.

Campbell, Peter. *French Electoral System and Elections since 1789.* London: Frederick A. Praeger, 1965.

Chapman, Brian. *Introduction to French Local Government.* London: George Allen and Unwin, 1953.

————. *The Prefect and Provincial France.* London: George Allen and Unwin, 1955.

Charléty, S. *La Restauration. Histoire de la France contemporaine,* edited by Ernst Lavisse, vol. 4. Paris: Libraire Hachette, 1921.

————. *La Monarchie de Juillet. Histoire de la France contemporaine,* edited by Ernst Lavisse, vol. 5. Paris: Libraire Hachette, 1921.

Chevallier, J. J. *Histoire des institutions et des régimes politiques de la France moderne, 1789–1958.* Paris: Libraire Dalloz, 1967.

Cobb, Richard. *The Police and the People: French Popular Protest, 1789–1820.* Oxford: Oxford University Press, 1970.

Cobban, Alfred. *The Social Interpretation of the French Revolution.* Cambridge: Cambridge University Press, 1965.

Crauffon, Jehan. *La Chambre des Députés sous la Restauration.* Paris: V. Girard et E. Brière, 1908.

Daumard, Adeline. *La bourgeoisie parisienne de 1815 à 1848.* Paris: S.E.V.P.E.N., 1963.

Ford, Franklin. *Robe and Sword.* New York: Harper and Row, 1965.

Girard, Louis. *Le libéralisme en France de 1814 à 1848.* Paris: Centre de documentation universitaire, 1967.

————. *La garde nationale, 1814–1871.* Paris: Libraire Plon, 1964.

Gobert, Adrienne. *L'opposition des assemblées pendant le Consulat.* Paris: Ernest Sagot et Cie, 1925.

Godechot, Jacques. *Les institutions de la France sous la Révolution et l'Empire.* Paris: Presses Universitaires de France, 1968.

Greer, Donald. *The Incidence of the Emigration During the French Revolution.* Gloucester, Mass.: Peter Smith, 1966.

————. *The Incidence of the Terror During the French Revolution.* Gloucester, Mass.: Peter Smith, 1966.

Gruder, Vivian R. *The Royal Provincial Intendants.* Ithaca: Cornell University Press, 1968.

Kent, Sherman. *Electoral Procedures under Louis-Philippe.* New Haven: Yale University Press, 1937.

Lavisse, Ernst. *See* Charléty, S.

Lefebvre, Georges. *The French Revolution.* 2 vols. New York: Columbia University Press, 1962.

————. *Napoléon.* Paris: Presses Universitaires de France, 1965.

Leuilliot, Paul. *L'Alsace au début du XIXe siècle.* 3 vols. Paris: S.E.V.P.E.N., 1959.

Lhomme, Jean. *La grande bourgeoisie au pouvoir, 1830–1880.* Paris: Presses Universitaires de France, 1960.

Mellon, Stanley. *The Political Uses of History.* Stanford: Stanford University Press, 1958.

Meuriot, Paul. *La population et les lois électorales en France de 1789 à nos jours.* Nancy: Berger-Levrault, 1916.

Patrick, Alison Kary Houston. "The French National Convention of 1792–1793: A Study of Political Alignments." Dissertation, University of Melbourne, 1969.

Pinkney, David H. *The French Revolution of 1830.* Princeton: Princeton University Press, 1972.

Ponteil, Felix. *L'éveil des nationalités et le mouvement libéral, 1815–1848.* Paris: Presses Universitaires de France, 1968.

————. *Les institutions de la France de 1814 à 1870.* Paris: Presses Universitaires de France, 1966.

Pouthas, Charles. *Guizot pendant la Restauration.* Paris: Libraire Plon, 1923.

Rémond, René. *The Right Wing in France from 1815 to De Gaulle.* Philadelphia: University of Pennsylvania Press, 1966.

Resnick, Daniel P. *The White Terror and the Political Reaction after Waterloo.* Cambridge: Harvard University Press, 1966.

Richardson, Nicholas. *The French Prefectoral Corps, 1814–1830.* Cambridge: Cambridge University Press, 1966.

Robin, Régine. *La Société française en 1789: Semur-en-Auxois.* Paris: Libraire Plon, 1970.

Sée, Henri. *La vie économique de la France sous la monarchie censitaire (1815–1848).* Paris: Libraire Felix Alcan, 1927.

Soltau, Roger Henry. *French Political Thought in the Nineteenth Century.* New York: Russell and Russell, 1959.

Stewart, John Hall. *The Restoration Era, 1814–1830.* Princeton: D. Van Nostrand and Co., 1968.

Tudesq, André-Jean. *Les conseillers généraux en France au temps de Guizot. 1840–1848.* Paris: Libraire Armand Colin, 1967.

————. *Les grands notables en France, 1840–1848.* Paris: Presses Universitaires de France, 1964.

Vidalenc, Jean. *Le Département de l'Eure sous la monarchie constitutionnelle, 1814–1848.* Paris: Marcel Rivière et Cie, 1952.

————. *Les émigrés français, 1789–1825.* Caen: Association des Publications de la faculté, Lettres et Sciences Humaines, Université de Caen, 1963.

————. *La société française de 1815 à 1848: Le peuple des campagnes.* Paris: Marcel Rivière et Cie, 1970.

Weil, Georges-Denis. *Les élections législative depuis 1789.* Paris: Felix Alcan, 1895.

Wright, Gordon. *France in Modern Times*. Chicago: Rand Mc-
    Nally, 1960.

Secondary Works on Statistical Analysis

Cattell, Raymond B. *Factor Analysis*. New York: Harper and
    Brothers, 1952.
Frutcher, Benjamin. *Introduction to Factor Analysis*. Princeton:
    D. Van Nostrand Co., 1954.
Ghiselli, Edwin E. *Theory of Psychological Measurement*. New
    York: McGraw-Hill, 1964.
Hays, William L. *Statistics*. New York: Holt, Rinehart, and
    Winston, 1963.
Tryon, Robert C., and Daniel E. Bailey. *Cluster Analysis*. New
    York: McGraw-Hill, 1970.
Walker, Helen M., and Joseph Lev. *Elementary Statistical Meth-
    ods*. Rev. ed. New York: Holt, Rinehart, and Winston, 1958.
Zeisel, Hans. *Say It with Figures*. New York: Harper and Row,
    1968.

Articles

Ameye, J. "La bourgeoisie tourquennoise sous la monarchie
    censitaire." *Revue du Nord* 47 (January–March 1965): 15–28.
Artz, Frederick B. "The Electoral System in France during the
    Bourbon Restoration, 1815–1830." *Journal of Modern History*
    1 (June 1929): 205–19.
Bécarud. "La noblesse dans les chambres, 1815–48." *Revue
    internationale d'histoire politique et constitutionnelle* (July–
    December 1953).
Bouyaux, P. "Les 'six cents plus imposés' du département de la
    Haute-Garonne en l'An X." *Annales du Midi* 70 (July 1958):
    317–27.
Cobban, Alfred. "The 'Middle Class' in France, 1815–1848."
    French Historical Studies 5 (Spring 1967): 41–52.
Daumard, Adeline. "Une réference pour l'étude des sociétés
    urbaines en France aux XVIIIe et XIXe siècles. Project de
    code socio-professional." *Revue d'histoire moderne et con-
    temporaine* 10 (July–September 1963): 185–210.
———. "Structures sociales et classement socio-professional."
    Revue historique 227 (January–March 1962): 139–54.

Dawson, Philip. "The Bourgeoisie de Robe in 1789." *French Historical Studies* 4 (Spring 1965): 1–22.

Egret, Jean. "L'aristocratic parlementaire française à la fin de l'Ancien régime." *Revue historique* 208 (July–September 1952:) 1–14.

Goueffon, Jean. "Contribution à l'étude des députés du Loiret sous la Restauration." *Information historique* 25 (November–December 1963): 202–7.

Gruner, Shirley. "The Revolution of July 1830 and the Expression 'Bourgeoisie.' " *The Historical Journal* 11 (1968): 462–471.

Higonnet, Patrick B. "La composition de la Chambre des Députés de 1827 à 1831." *Revue historique* 239 (April–June 1968): 351–75.

Higonnet, Patrick B., and Trevor B. "Class Corruption and Politics in the French Chamber of Deputies, 1846–1848." *French Historical Studies* 5 (Fall 1967): 204–24.

Kelly, George A. "Liberalism and Aristocracy in the French Restoration." *Journal of the History of Ideas* 26 (October–December 1965): 509–30.

Mater, André. "Le groupement régional des partis politiques à la fin de la Restauration." *La Révolution française* 42 (1902): 406–63.

Mazayer, Louis. "Catégories d'age et groupes sociaux des jeunes génerations française de 1830." *Annales d'histoire économique et sociale* (No. 53, September 1938): 385–419.

O'Boyle, Lenore. "The Middle Class in Western Europe, 1815–1848." *American Historical Review* 71 (April 1966): 826–45.

Pouthas, Charles. "Les ministères de Louis-Philippe." *Revue d'histoire moderne et contemporaine* 1 (April–June 1954): 102–30.

————. "La ré-organisation du Ministère de l'Intérieur et la reconstitution de l'administration préfectorale par Guizot en 1830." *Revue d'histoire moderne et contemporaine* 9 (October–December 1962): 241–64.

Roche, D., and M. Vovelle. "Bourgeois, Rentiers, and Property Owners: Elements for Defining a Social Category at the End of the Eighteenth Century." In *New Perspectives on the French Revolution*, edited by Jeffry Kaplow, New York, 1965 (pp. 25–46).

Roussel, Charles. "La candidature officielle sous la Restauration: Une élection en 1820." *Revue politique et parlementaire*
19 (February 1899): 351–69.
Soutadé-Rouger. "Les notables en France sous la Restauration,
1815–1830." *Revue d'histoire économique et sociale* 38 (1960):
98–110.
Taylor, George V. "Noncapitalist Wealth and the Origins of
the French Revolution." *American Historical Review* 72 (January 1967): 469–96.
Tudesq, André-Jean. "Une catégorie dirigeante: les grands notables sous la Monarchie de Juillet," *Bulletin de la société
d'histoire moderne* (no. 1, 1966).
Welschinger, Henri. "Tribuns, Députés, Sénateurs, 1804–1810."
Revue hebdomadaire 6 (1898): 246–63.

INDEX